Teach'n Beginning Defensive Volleyball Drills, Plays, and Games Free Flow Handbook

By Bob Swope
Series 5, Vol. 18 Free Flow Paperback Edition
Copyright 2014 Bob Swope

ISBN 13: 9780991406630

TABLE OF CONTENTS

Note:
This book is a combination of many techniques in several of our books, "Teach'n Volleyball," and "Youth Volleyball Drills and Plays."

1. Warning

If your kids, players on your team, or the participants have any physically limiting conditions, bleeding disorder, high blood pressure, any kind of heart condition, pregnancy or any other condition that may limit them physically, you should have them check with their doctor before letting them participate in any of the drills, plays, games, activities, or exercises discussed in this book.

Be sure participants in these drills, plays, games, or exercises that might even accidentally make hard contact with any of the other participants are all approximately of the same weight and size to avoid a possible accidental serious injury.

All of the drills, plays, exercises, and games for kids discussed in this book should be supervised by a competent adult, coach, or a professional using all the required equipment and safety procedures. **AUTHOR ASSUMES NO LIABILITY FOR ANY ACCIDENTAL INJURY OR EVEN DEATH THAT MAY RESULT FROM USING ANY OF THE VOLLEYBALL TECHNIQUES, DRILLS, OR ACTIVITIES, DISCUSSED IN THIS BOOK.**

Extra care and caution should be taken with any of the drills in this book where players may accidentally get hit with a spiked Volleyball because that may be the more dangerous thing to watch for. Concussions can happen. Occasionally kids will have bruised knees or a broken body part. Remove them and have them immediately checked out by a doctor. Also watch for over exertion (heat stroke and heart problems) to any of your kids or players out on the court that get overheated for some reason. Having a "defibrillator" near by would be a big help in case something like that happens.

Bob Swope
Jacobob Press LLC
Publisher

2. Introduction

My Interest and Intent

Occasionally youth Volleyball coaches have asked me about basic defensive Volleyball drills, plays, strategies, tactics and games that would be good to have all in one book, to use for training purposes. This handbook is intended to be a supplemental book to my "Teach'n Volleyball" book. This book is orientated more for the beginner volleyball coach, rather than parents at home teaching fundamentals. However, parents at home can help their kids by getting them to work on the drills, plays, tactics, and strategies in this book while at home. We will break this down into where your players are in their training, and what they are doing at that stage of their training.

Also what drills, strategies, plays and tactics to use that will accomplish your goals in teaching them. My suggestion is use the time you have each week to maximize what you want to teach. For the younger 6 -11 years of age kids it's better to break practice drills down into more than one small group to keep everyone busy so that they don't get bored. This is not always easy to do because many coaches only want things done their way, and they don't always trust a helper assistant to do it their way. However, sooner or later you need to trust assistants to help get more done. It's in the best interest of the kids because it's all about the kids not you.

3. Discussion

Training Sessions

Some of the beginning volleyball practices I've seen will only last about an hour. This is where one coach may have the whole group. I have seen coaches spending 15 to 20 minutes warming up, stretching, running and things like that. That leaves only 45 or so minutes to instruct, not counting the water breaks. And it's not-always one-on one instruction. This means you need to manage your time efficiently. You should limit the warm-up and stretching, so you can utilize the maximum amount of practice time. Of course if you have more time its not a problem. The other thing that is important is how many times a week is your practice. If it's only 1 day a week, you better sit down and make a schedule, so you can cover all the things they need to learn. Then follow it. If you have more time, like two hours, you can teach even more fundamentals by adding to our "Sample Practice Schedules" at the back of the book.

Time

Generally, keep your training time to around 10 to 15 minutes per drill being explained, especially if you have a group unless otherwise noted. Now here is where your training techniques may need to change. If you have a helper you can split into two groups. As an example, you might be teaching "blocking" and your assistant "digging and saving." Then after 10 to 15 minutes you switch or rotate groups. This is because traditionally there is a lot of techniques to teach to beginning kids. In other words always keep your kids busy doing something at all times except for water breaks. Don't have any kids just standing around waiting because there is only one coach. You don't get as much teaching in that way, within any one practice. Also young kids traditionally get bored easily if you don't keep them busy for the entire training session.

Session Suggestions

I suggest getting as many assistant coaches as you can, then explain to them individually what they are responsible for teaching at their station or group. Tell your staff to learn all the kids names the first day if possible because it helps build a relationship. Time wise plan your whole practice session. The kids will learn more in the short periods of time you have for teaching each day or week. As for the teaching methods we suggest using the "IDEA" slogan approach. **I**ntroduce, **D**emonstrate, **E**xplain what you are teaching, and **A**ttend (answer any question-show them how) to all the players in the group.

The Opponent
If it's possible, it could be beneficial to understand what tendencies your opponent has. Your players need to learn how to quickly figure out what their opponent is doing against them offensively on the other side of the net. Your players should recognize the importance of this strategy, especially after playing an opponent more than once. Here is a little strategy you can employ as their coach. Keep a small pad of paper in your pocket and take notes. Look for weaknesses then when it's game time you can pick the defensive strategies that will attack, counterattack, and defeat what the opponent is doing offensively. Start teaching your young players to have a game plan before they go into a game then test them to make sure and remember what it is. Also have one or two back up plans in case your first plan didn't work and you need to change plans and tactics quickly. And have signals or code words for each one.

Pre Practice/Game Warm Up
Before your team starts to practice or get in a game they need to go through a little warm up to get their muscles warmed up and stretched out. We will give you a nice little quick warm up routine to use. 10 minutes should do it. They need to do this when they first get to the practice. Once your kids learn it, they can do it on their own as a group. If you can teach them to do this well, and look good at it, your opponent may be impressed or intimidated by your teams discipline and focus if they see your team doing this. The organized warm up may put you at a slight advantage, as your opponent's may be a little psyched out.

Drills
I am going to refer to the drills as "Skill Training Activities" because that's what they really are. Also I am going to throw in a newer term now being used a lot. It is called "Core Training." What it does is train their body to automatically make certain moves that will make them a better player. Drills will be organized by *"numbers"* so that

your assistant coaches can use them and become more familiar with them that way. This way you are all on the same page as they say.

Techniques

Techniques are the most important fundamental things to learn. For easy reference the techniques will be organized by *"numbers"* also. They will be arranged in the different defensive techniques and tactics. Each technique or tactic will have a short explanation for how it is supposed to work, strong points, what it is designed to accomplish.

Game Type Scrimmages

It's a good idea to introduce game type scrimmages once in a while. Beginners sometimes have a tendency to get bored with constant drilling. They want to see what it's like to go out and play in a game against an actual opponent. You need to referee these games though just like in a real game. Just don't get frustrated by expecting perfect play by beginners. Have several spotters, each watching some particular aspect of their de
fensive play, and taking notes. As they get better you can be more particular about calling scores and penalties.

Core Training Games

Many coaches over the years have asked me to give them some "core training" games they can have the kids play once in a while at practices. Not just any games though, but games that will help develop some part of their "core training" and "muscle memory" in a particular skill. So we are adding some games that will do just that. For easy reference these games will be organized by *"numbers"* also. Some of the time it's hard for coaches to buy into these games, but the more you play them, the more you will see your player's agility, speed and skills improving. Each game will have a short explanation for how it is supposed to work, strong points, and what the game is designed to accomplish.

General Strategies and Tactics

The first general strategy I recommend is "have a game plan" to match your team with their opponent. Try to watch the opponent warming up, and make some notes. Remember though these are only kids, so coach accordingly with your strategies and tactics if you are working with kids 7-11 years of age. You know the old "KISS" (Keep-It-Simple-Stupid) phrase. In volleyball it is not structured as say football with all its many plays. However, each player does have a roll to play depending on their position on the court. For beginners it's important to teach them in detail what their individual role is at each position and how it relates to the team. For the in-depth strategies see the full "Strategies" section.

4. Warm Up Exercises

I'm going to give you a quick warm up routine your players can use to get warmed up and their muscles stretched. That's all young kids really need. Teach your players how to do these group exercises all by themselves as a group. It will be easier that way. Here is an idea I have used before. When you are warming up your team, you can try this. Have your captain or a respected teammate stand in front of the group, and lead the routine. Teach your players to count slowly and out loud. The team alternates counting, when the leaders yell. "One," the group yells, "Two on the next rep," etc. You only need to do six reps of each exercise. It's also a "psyche out" for any opponent's that may be watching. And you may need this edge if the opponent's are more experienced or have stronger players. You are only looking at about 10 minutes to go through these.

The Simple Routine
1. Start by doing 10 jumping jacks to get their muscles warmed up.
2. Next slowly do 6 "seated hamstring/quadriceps stretches.
3. Next slowly do 3 pelvic stretches on each side, holding for 3 seconds between them.

4. Next slowly do 6 push forward pull back ankle stretches.
5. Next slowly do 3 front quadriceps stretches on both thighs, leaning forward and holding for 3 seconds between them.
6. Next slowly do 6 rear shoulder stretches, holding for 3 seconds.
7. Next slowly do 3 front shoulder stretches on each shoulder, holding for 3 seconds between them.
8. Last use a teammate to lean on, or find a wall, and slowly do 3 calf stretches on each leg, holding it for 3 seconds between each rep.

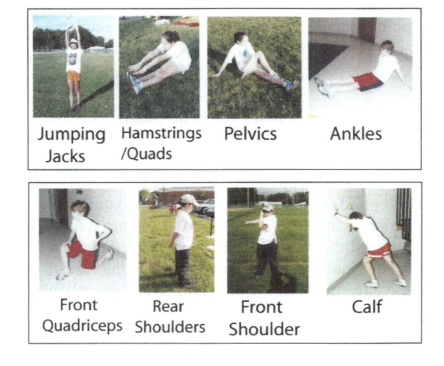

Jumping Jacks   Hamstrings/Quads   Pelvics   Ankles

Front Quadriceps   Rear Shoulders   Front Shoulder   Calf

<u>5. Where They Play on the Court</u>

This is basically for new beginning coaches without a lot of experience in volleyball. In youth volleyball there are usually 6 players and positions on the volleyball court for each team (side). In some places they will occasionally play 3 vs 3 volleyball. And in beach volleyball they will sometimes play 2 vs 2 volleyball. In this book we will only cover 6 vs 6 youth volleyball because it is the most popular. Volleyball is not like some of the other sports that play on a court. They start out arranged in a certain order at the time of the serve, which starts out play *(SEE DIAGRAM 1)*.

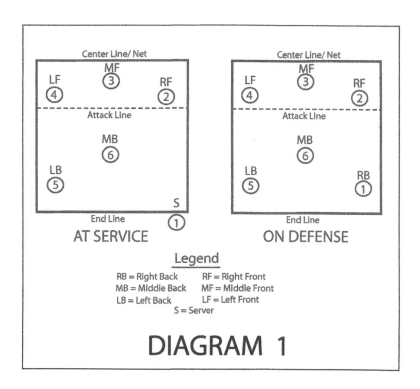

And after the point has been made each player rotates around clockwise to the next position. As an example, No.1 moves to No. 6, No.2 moves to No. 1. At the serve the server usually is right behind the end line. All the other players have to be within the court lines until the ball has been served. In youth volleyball there are 6 players on the court for defensive play. There are many different locations where the coach may move them up or back once the ball is in play. We will just give you the required positions as of when they start play.

6. Defensive Skill Training Activities

Note: ALL ACTIVITIES will be numbered for "EASY " reference.

The defensive drills will cover all the types of skills that young kids learning to play defensive volleyball need to know to get started of on the right foot. Some are "core training' and most all involve "muscle memory" training. They train the body, arms, legs and feet of your players to make certain moves and decisions that will make them a better player. Defensive volleyball players need to be poised and patient. Volleyball is a little more complex than a beginner would expect.

The skill activities are numbered so that you can have your assistant coach(s) use them and become more familiar with them for reference purposes. These skill activities will cover the very basic fundamentals like footwork, digging, blocking, the sprawl technique, rebounding, pursuing and saving. We will also try to cover some of the little special techniques that will help them. The plan is stay with small training groups, where you or one of your coaches is teaching one of theses skills. Keep the time period short, maybe 10 to 15 minutes depending on the size of your team and how much practice time you have. Then blow a whistle and one group moves over to the other group. The key is keep repeating the training over and over every few weeks, but keep it moving around to different techniques. Not only the same ones all the time.

Modern volleyball training, and conditioning, is advancing all the time. In this book we will try to follow the latest recommended techniques, and tailor them for the younger kids. I will break the drills and skill training down into the fundamental categories, and how they relate to what you want to teach. We will use picture figures, and diagrams as much as possible, to eliminate some of the confusion for all helping fathers, and some mothers, who may never have played the game of volleyball. So, bear with us, those of you that have played a lot of volleyball. This book was basically written as a reference book for beginners, both parents, coaches, and the kids.

The size of your groups will depend on how many kids you have at your training session, and how many instructors (coaches) you have. As an example if you have 12 kids on your team, then you could have 2 groups of 6. Then you would need 2 stations and at least one instructor, coach, or parent per group. The bigger your group is though the more problems you will have. Smaller groups mean more touches, and more teaching control on you or your coaches part. However, some drills may need to be combined into the whole team in order to teach similar techniques more smoothly and quicker to the team as a whole. If you can find them, have an instructor and an assistant at each station, then show them what to do.

Most coaches don't like to do this even if they may need to because of a large group size, but using parents as assistants and showing them exactly what you want them to do can work. I do this all the time and it works great for me with young kids. Parents are usually just sitting around watching with nothing to do anyway, so why not get them involved and put them to work. There is always some of them that are willing to help. You would be surprised at how many parents are willing to help, not a lot but quite a few. And that's all you need. The key is just give them a simple task then show them *EXACTLY* what you want them to do.

Here is another technique that works great with young kids. They have a short attention span. So when you need to talk to all of them, then make them all sit down cross legged on the ground in a semi circle in front of you. When you do it this way, they have less of a tendency to mess around, especially with boys, who tend talk too much when you are talking. Don't let them stand up, that's when the listening usually tends to stop and distractions set in.

Additional Help for Activities

If you are a beginning coach, and you are having trouble understanding how to implement these offensive activities in more detail, get a copy of the "Teach'n Volleyball" book. This is our teaching book for Volleyball, and it goes into a little more detail on certain things and exactly how to teach kids the particular skill we are discussing.

Legend for All Diagrams

(Unless otherwise spelled out in the diagram or section)

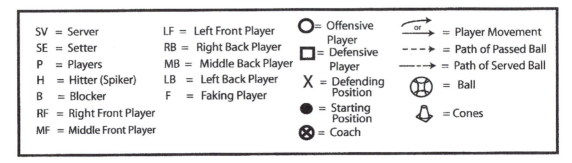

SV = Server	LF = Left Front Player	O = Offensive Player
SE = Setter	RB = Right Back Player	□ = Defensive Player
P = Players	MB = Middle Back Player	X = Defending Position
H = Hitter (Spiker)	LB = Left Back Player	● = Starting Position
B = Blocker	F = Faking Player	⊗ = Coach
RF = Right Front Player		
MF = Middle Front Player		

→ or → = Player Movement
- - - ► = Path of Passed Ball
----- ► = Path of Served Ball
⊕ = Ball
♟ = Cones

7. Individual Footwork and Movement Techniques

The first fundamental your players need to learn is the basic footwork and movements in volleyball. They have to do them enough so they become a habit with them (muscular memory). These drills are basically to teach them to move automatically to the ball. The footwork and movements put the player in the right position to execute whatever skill they need, to make a play on the ball. The "hop" part of the technique is probably the hardest part for young kids to learn. They usually make too small of a "hop," or none at all. There are four basic fundamental movements. Leap hopping, slide stepping, crossover stepping, and the blocking approach steps. The crossover step is a blocking footwork move. What this means is you probably don't need to teach this move until your players can get their hands over the top of the net. We will break all the movements down separately. Eventually though your players will need to learn all of them.

Skill Activity No. 25, 26- The Leap Hopping Technique
Object of the Activity:
Teach all your players how to move quickly and get into a balanced position by using leap hopping.
What you will need:
You will need some room on a back corner of the court or in front of the net, 2 coaches, and a whistle.
The Basics are:
   A. This is basically taking one step forward with the *right* foot, followed quickly with a jump up forward hop coming down in a balanced position on the *left* foot, and almost simultaneously followed by the *right* foot. It should make a step "pop," then a quick "pop"- "pop" sound on the floor as the feet come down each time *(SEE FIGURE 25-A)*.
   B. Next take a step backward with the *right* foot, followed quickly with a jump up backward hop coming down in a balanced position on the *left* foot, and almost simultaneously followed by the *right* foot. It should make a step "pop," then a quick "pop"- "pop" sound on the floor as the feet come down each time *(SEE FIGURE 25-B)*.
   C. This is basically taking one step forward with the *left* foot, followed quickly with a jump up forward hop coming down in a balanced position on the *right* foot, and almost simultaneously followed by the *left* foot. It should make a step "pop," then a quick "pop"- "pop" sound on the floor as the feet come down each time *(SEE FIGURE 25-C)*.

D. Next take a step backward with the _left_ foot, followed quickly with a jump up backward hop coming down in a balanced position on the _right_ foot, and almost simultaneously followed by the _left_ foot. It should make a step "pop," then a quick "pop"- "pop" sound on the floor as the feet come down each time *(SEE FIGURE 25-D)*.

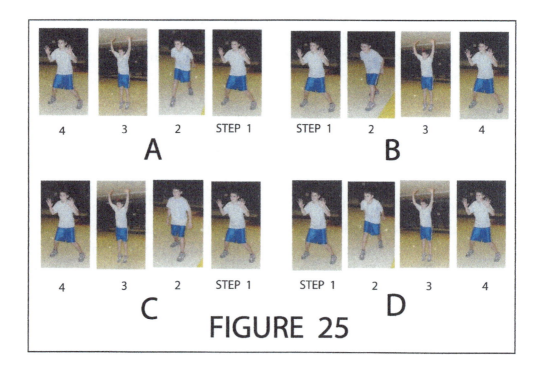

4	3	2	STEP 1		STEP 1	2	3	4
		A					**B**	

4	3	2	STEP 1		STEP 1	2	3	4
	C					**D**		

FIGURE 25

Working the Activity:

This can be practiced out in the back yard, but it's better to work on a driveway, or a gym floor. The reason is, you can hear the "pops" especially on the gym floor as the feet come down. Then you know they are doing it correctly. If they don't jump up and hop, you will not hear the "pops" of the feet. Have them get into a ready position first *(SEE FIGURE 26),* then go through the _right_ foot leap hops in slow motion at least 5 times each at a session, forward then backward. Next have them go through the _left_ foot leap hops in slow

14

motion at least 5 times each at a session, forward then backward *(SEE FIGURE 25)*. Then they speed it up as they get better.

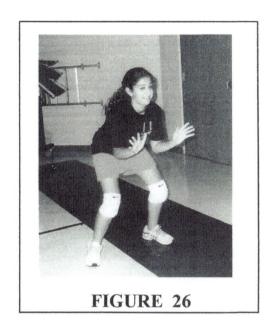

FIGURE 26

Emphasize;
Jumping up hopping and hearing the popping.
Run the Activity:
Run this activity quickly over and over for about 10-15 minutes.

Skill Activity No. 27- The Slide Stepping Technique
Object of the Activity:
Teach all your players how to move sideways quickly by using the slide stepping technique.
What you will need:
You will need some room on a back corner of the court or in front of the net, 2 coaches, and a whistle.
The Basics are:
    A. This is basically taking a step to the <u>right</u> with the right foot, then sliding the left foot over to it. Next make a short step

"hop" over to the right, with the right foot first, coming down in a balanced position with the feet under the shoulders *(SEE FIGURE 27-GOING RIGHT)*.

B. Next take a step to the *left* with the left foot, then sliding the right foot over to it. Next make a short step "hop" over to the left, with the left foot first, coming down in a balanced position with the feet under the shoulders *(SEE FIGURE 27-GOING LEFT)*. Doing this in slow motion first may help.

GOING RIGHT

GOING LEFT

FIGURE 27

Working the Activity:

This can be practiced out in the back yard, but it's better to work on a driveway, or a gym floor. The reason is, you can hear the "pops" when the feet come down, especially on the gym floor. Then you know they are doing it correctly. If they don't jump up and hop, you will not hear the "pops" of the feet. Have them get into a ready position first *(SEE FIGURE 26),* then go through the slide step in slow motion to the *right* first for at least 5 times a session. Next have them go through the slide step in slow motion to the *left* for at least 5 times a session *(SEE FIGURE 27)*. Then speed it up as they get better.

16

Emphasize;
Jumping up, going sideways and hearing the popping.
Run the Activity:
Run this activity quickly over and over for about 10-15 minutes.

Skill Activity No. 28- The Crossover Stepping Technique
Object of the Activity:
Teach all your players how to move sideways quickly by using the cross over stepping technique.
What you will need:
You will need some room on a back corner of the court or in front of the net, 2 coaches, and a whistle.
The Basics are:
- A. To go to the right, turn to the right with the body, and open to the right with the right foot turning it 90 degrees to the right. Next take a quick big crossover step in front with the left foot. Step and swing the right leg around to the front, squaring the body to the front, all in one move *(SEE FIGURE 28-A)*.
- B. To go to the left, turn to the left with the body, and open to the left with the left foot turning it 90 degrees to the left. Next take a quick big crossover step in front with the right foot. Step and swing the left leg around to the front, squaring the body to the front, all in one move *(SEE FIGURE 28-B)*.

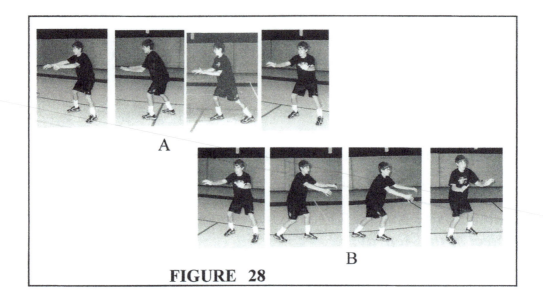

FIGURE 28

Working the Activity:
This can be practiced out in the back yard, but it's better to work on a driveway, or a gym floor. The reason is, you can hear a slight "pop" when the feet come down, especially on the gym floor. Then you know they are doing it correctly. If they don't jump up at least a little bit you won't hear the "pop" of the feet. Have them get into a ready position first *(SEE FIGURE 26),* then go through the crossover step to the <u>right</u> for at least 5 times a session. Next have them go through the crossover step to the <u>left</u> for at least 5 times a session *(SEE FIGURE 28)*.

Emphasize;
Going through the move in slow motion then crossing the feet over, going sideways, and hearing the slight popping.

Run the Activity:
Run this activity quickly over and over for about 10-15 minutes.

Team Footwork Drills

These are drills you can run with the whole team involved. You keep running these drills every once in a while to sharpen up the footwork of all your players.

The Footwork Drill (No. 300)
Object of the Activity:
Teach all your players to further sharpen up all their footwork skill moves.
What you will need:
You will need a whole half court, 2 coaches, and a whistle.
The Basics are:
This is sharpening up their footwork skills for "leap hopping," "Slide Stepping," "Crossover Stepping," "The 2, 3 , and 4 Step Spike Approach," and the "Side Step Spike Approach."

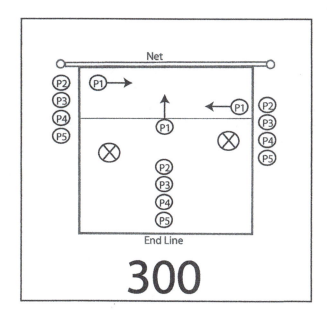

Working the Activity:

Have your players line up in 3 groups. Player P1 in the center group starts out on the whistle. They do 1 or 2 "leap hops" straight ahead then go to the end of the line one their right. Coach blows their whistle and player P1 in the line on the left does "slide steps" all the way across to the other side then goes to the end of the line in the middle. Coach blows their whistle again and player P1 on the line on the right does a "crossover" step all the way to the other side than goes to the end of the line on the left side.

This is how players rotate and do a different step each time. After everyone has been through these 3 moves once coach blows their and everyone stops. Now coach picks 3 different footwork moves for each of the 3 lines. The slide and side stepping moves come from the sides, the leap hopping and the straight ahead spike approach moves come from the middle line. If players are having trouble with the footwork have the roving coach pull them aside and work with them on their moves. This way the drill keeps going.

8. Individual Digging Techniques

The dig is saving technique for low spike hit. This is because this technique is an instantaneous response to receiving, then passing, a fast and hard to get to ball. There is a little time for movement in the forearm pass, but not the "dig." There are various corrections you can use to help your player become a better "digger." We will touch on these so you can help them by observing where their digs are going, compared to where they should have gone.

Skill Activity No. 56, 57- The Dig Technique
Object of the Drill:
Teach your players how to dig hard hit balls.

What you will Need:

You will need a full court with a net to work on, a bucket of balls, 2 coaches, and a whistle.

The Basics Are:

This is taking the forearm pass technique and altering it a little to become what is called a "dig". I suspect the technique got its name from watching a player go down real low with their hands, then sort of scooping or digging underneath the ball to keep it from hitting the floor. Teach your son or daughter to let the ball go as low as possible, which will give them just fractions of a second of more time to react. What they have to learn how to do is absorb the force of the ball by dropping the forearms down just as the ball makes contact. This is going to be hard for the little kids to learn. It will take lots of trial and error work with them to learn how to do this. Don't give up on them though because they can learn how to perform this technique. It's just going to take lots of patience on your part coach, mom, or dad, along with many repetitions. They should also flex and stiffen their elbows, and just flick the wrists, when the ball makes contact. At the same time their body needs dip way down low *(SEE FIGURE 56)*. This will make the ball get up in the air. Have them learn to direct the ball as close as possible to the front center of the court, in front of the net.

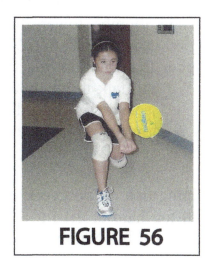

FIGURE 56

Working the Activity:

You can practice this technique out in the back yard, but the court is a better place. And you really do need a net to get the actual feeling of the ball coming hard over the top of the net though. Have them go any place in the back row and get into the "ready" position *(SEE FIGURE 26)*. When they see the ball is about to be hit, they put their thumbs together in the forearm pass hands position *(SEE FIGURE 53)*. The next thing is, they have to step right at the ball with either foot *(SEE FIGURE 57-A)*. Which foot goes forward will depend on which side of them the ball is coming from. The next important thing to do is have them get their hips lower than the ball.

Teach them how to maneuver so that the ball comes down inside of their knees if possible. To work on this technique they are going to have to work on their quickness, agility, and flexibility drills. What they want to do is get the thumbs scooped under the ball just before contact. This way the ball will rebound off the wrists *(SEE FIGURE 57-B)*. They will have to learn to be careful making this move though, by flexing and pointing the thumbs down. If they point the thumbs up, the ball can hit on the end of the thumbs and possibly dislocate or injure them. This is especially true with the little kids and beginners. When you get the hands and thumbs scooped under the ball, it will normally put back spin on it. However they must keep the hands and thumbs lower than the elbows so that the forearms are angled down *(SEE FIGURE 57-B)*. If the hands are even with, or higher than the elbows, then the ball can go up and over their head. We will talk more about this in the correction drill section next. The accuracy and direction of the "dig" is accomplished by pointing the thumbs in the direction you want the ball to go in.

Here is three training tips for you coach, mom, or dad. Number **one** *do not* hit the ball too hard at the little kids and beginners. It really discourages them quickly. Number **two**, walk them through the body, feet, and hands position slowly until they catch on. Like step out and dip to the right, then to the left. Number **three**, let some air out of the ball for the little kids, so the hard hit balls don't sting so much on their forearms, or they can wear long sleeve shirts. They should practice this drill at least 3 times to the right, and 3 times to the left at a training session.

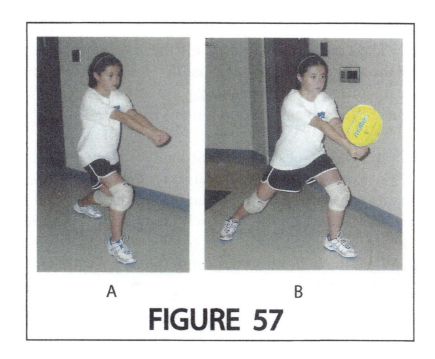

A   B

FIGURE 57

Emphasize:
Stress getting low and getting their hands under the ball
Run this drill:
Run it for only 15 minutes rapidly, then have the group move to the next station or a different drill.

Skill Activity No. 42- Dig Error and Corrections
The Basics are:
The reason I am adding this section in the drills is, I want you as coaches and parents to be able to correct their "dig" technique errors while they are trying to learn because this is going to be hard for the little kids. The technique is going to be very hard to teach young kids, and beginners, to perform successfully. So at least you will be able to watch them, and correct what they might be doing wrong. When the error is having the ball go straight up, or back over their head. The correction is, don't hit the ball hard with their forearms. Stop the arms at contact and use a "poking" type move at the ball. Have them let the ball go down lower to the waist level, and keep their shelf (arms) angled down more in front.

When the ball comes off of their hands to low and won't go over the net. *The correction is*, they have to get lower under the ball and scoop it more with the shelf (hands). To do this, have them go all the way down and touch the floor with their hands. Also have them bend the knees more, and keep their back straight as they go down for the ball. When the ball, hit to the center court position, does not get up in the air high enough (2 or 3 feet above the top of the net) for the setter; The correction is, have them flex and stiffen their arms, then just flick their wrists at the ball. All of these corrections will help them if you coach, mom, or dad, keep watching them while they are training. Then not to "harshly," but continuously, keep making the corrections with them. All the time while they are practicing their "dig" technique, keep watching and correcting them as necessary.

Team Digging Drills

Note:
Digging is offensively associated because after digging the ball has to get to a setter in an attempt to set someone up to score.

Partner Digging Drill (No.45)

Object of the drill:

Learn to make digs when the ball is at a players feet, or a little away to either side of them.

What you will need:

You will need half a volleyball court with a net, a cart with balls, a coach, a whistle, a feeder, and a passer.

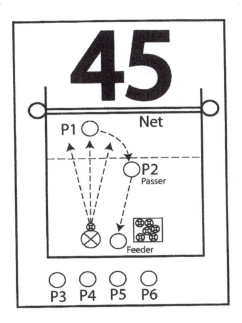

Working the drill:

This is going to be a tough drill for the younger kids. You may want to wait until they are 12 or older? Put a player P1 up in the front row, facing towards the backcourt. Coach stands facing them about 20 feet away, then overhand throws a ball directly at the feet of P1.

They need to get low and dig the ball over to P2, who passes to the feeder. The feeder always has a ball ready for coach, which keeps the drill moving. When P1 is comfortable digging straight at their feet then coach throws first to one side of P1 then the other. After about six throws, rotate and P3 steps up. After 12 throws rotate and switch the feeder and passer.

Emphasize;
Getting down low, and twisting the body to square up to throws to the side.

Run this drill:
Run the drill until each player gets their two cycles. After 30 minutes the group moves to the next station or a different drill.

The Dig and Cover Drill (No.46)

Object of the drill:
Learn to make digs when moving from back on defense then up to cover, then moving back to the back row.

What you will need:
You will need a volleyball court, a net, a cart with balls, a hitter/thrower, and a feeder.

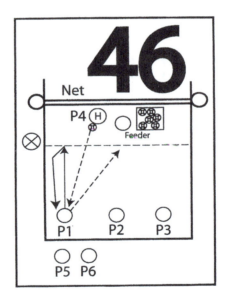

Working the drill:
Have one player P4 go up by the net with a ball. Then have three players P1, P2, and P3 spread out in the back row. P4 hits or throws the ball hard at P1 (touch one), they dig it towards the feeder. Then they run up, touch the ten foot line and run back to where they were.

26

Just as they get back P4 hits or throws another ball at them. They dig it toward the feeder (touch two), then run up touch the ten foot line, turn and go to the end of the line. Next P4 hits or throws to P2 and the drill repeats for two touches. Then they hit to P3 and they repeat the drill for two touches. The feeder always has a ball ready for the hitter so that the drill keeps moving.

Emphasize;
Getting down low to dig and twisting their body to square up to throws to the side. Players need to hustle, so they get more digs in.
Run this drill:
Run the drill until each player gets at least four touches. After 30 minutes the group moves to the next station or start a different drill.

The Scramble Dive and Dig Save Drill (No.47)
Object of the drill:
This drill will be hard on the younger kids. You may want to wait until they have more experience, or they are 12 years or older.
What you will need:
You will need a volleyball court, a net, 2 carts with balls, a thrower, and a catcher.
Working the drill:
Coach takes a ball and goes up on the sideline near the front row. Then have player P1 step up into the back court. Coach tosses the ball up high in the air towards the middle of the front row. P1 sprints to the ball, dives, and digs the ball to the catcher, then rolls over, gets up, and goes to the end of the line. Right away P2 steps up, and the toss and dig repeats. Catcher tosses the ball in the cart. When coaches cart is empty, they switch carts. This keeps the drill moving. This drill wants to move fast for about 7 minutes. Then everyone rests for a few minutes, then the drill goes again.

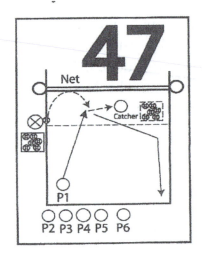

Emphasize;

Getting to the ball quickly diving and forearm digging the ball up in the air if possible to the catcher. Then executing the rollover and recover move, and getting up quickly. For safety purposes, make sure all your players have on elbow and knee pads for this drill.

Run this drill;

In 7 minute increments. After 30 minutes the group moves to the next station or starts a different drill.

The Teamwork Digging Drill (No.48)

Object of the drill:

Learn to make digs and use team work to get the ball back up to front court.

What you will need:

You will need a volleyball court, a net, a cart with balls, and a coach as a thrower.

Working the drill:

Coach gets a cart full of balls and goes up in the middle of the front row by the net. Then have three players P1, P2, and P3 spread out in the back row. Coach throws the ball hard at anyone of the players, they dig it towards one of the other players, who passes it back to the coach. Then they all go quickly back to their starting spot. Coach needs to mix up where they throw the ball, to make it harder for the players to dig the ball. After about 7 minutes, rotate in three new players.

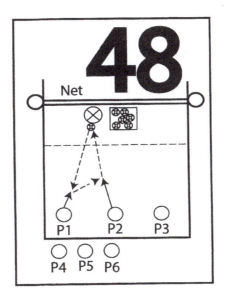

Emphasize;
Getting down low to dig, and getting a good dig up in the air that a teammate can get underneath to pass to coach.
Run this drill:
Run the drill until each player gets at least 3 minutes of work. After 30 minutes the group moves to the next station or starts a different drill.

9. The Sprawl/Roll Technique

The sprawl is a defensive move to extend your playing range, and to recover after attempting to retrieving (dig) a ball that is out of their forward reach. It is used when the player has reached as far as they can forward while on their feet, and must extend their body farther forward to make a play on the ball. This would be used whether you get to the ball or not though. It teaches them to go safely to the floor then get up quickly. The last part of this move is really another technique for controlled falling and court presence. Players need to learn how to perform this technique going to their right and to their left.

The roll is a another defensive move to extend your playing range, and to recover after attempting to retrieving (dig) a ball that is out of their forward reach. It is used when the player has reached as far as they can forward while on their feet, and must extend their body farther forward to make a play on the ball. This technique would be used whether you get to the ball or not though. It teaches them to go safely to the floor then roll over quickly and get to their feet again. The last part of this move is really another technique for controlled falling and court presence. Players need to learn how to perform this technique going to their right and to their left.

Skill Activity No. 53, 64- The Sprawl Technique
Object of the Drill:
Teach your players how to use the sprawl to save hard hit spikes out of their normal reach.
What you will Need:
You will need a full court with a net to work on, a bucket of balls, 2 coaches, and a whistle.
The Basics Are:
This is an extension of the "dig" technique. It starts out with your player in the ready position *(SEE FIGURE 64-A)*. Next they put their hands in the forearm pass position *(SEE FIGURE 53)*. To go to the right, they pivot on their left foot, turn to the right, and step way out 90 degrees. Following that, they bend way down and try to scoop both hands under the ball *(SEE FIGURE 64-B)*. If they can't get both hands under the ball, they have to go down and reach out

with the right hand and try to reach the ball. As they go down on their knees or stomach, they put the right knee on the floor, and slide the right foot out to the right. At the same time they put the left hand down on the floor to their left side, and reach way out straight ahead for the ball with the right arm *(SEE FIGURE 64-C)*.

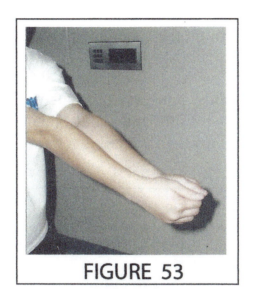

FIGURE 53

All they have to do to get back up is, push up with the left hand, bring their right leg back up underneath them and they are up quickly. To go to the left, everything is just flip flopped or opposite.

Working the activity:
To practice this technique, first make sure they have their knee pads on. And it might be a good idea to get them some elbow pads to practice in. You can practice this out in the back yard where there is some thick grass, or you can go out to a court someplace. First show, and explain to, your player what they will be doing. Next walk them through it slowly by the numbers, then speed it up little by little until they appear to be catching on how to do it.

Step 1, have them get into the "ready" position *(SEE FIGURE 64-A)*. *Step 2*, they move the hands into the forearm pass position *(SEE FIGURE 53)*. *Step 3*, to go to their right, they take a big step about 90 degrees out to their right using the right foot. *Step 4*, they make a swinging scoop move out to their right with their hands *(SEE FIGURE 64-B)*. *Step 5*, they put the left hand out next to their left shoulder to break their fall, kick the right leg out to their right, put the right knee down on the ground, and reach way out with the right hand for the ball, palm down *(SEE FIGURE 64-C)*. *Step 6*, They push up quickly with the left hand, bring the right leg back underneath their body, and get to their feet. To practice going to the left, take the big step to the left. They should make at least 3 moves to the right, and 3 moves to the left at a training session.

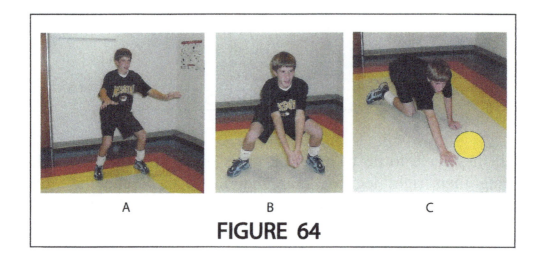

A   B   C
FIGURE 64

Emphasize;
Learning how to make a quick decision on when to go down to their knees or stomach, to get a hand under the ball.
Run the Activity:
Run this activity quickly over and over for about 30 minutes.

Skill Activity No. 65- The Roll Technique
Object of the Drill:
Teach your players how to use the roll technique after a save attempt.
What you will Need:
You will need half the court with a net to work on, a bucket of balls, 2 coaches, and a whistle.
The Basics Are:
This is also an extension of the "dig" technique. It starts out with your player in the ready position *(SEE FIGURE 65-A)*. Next they put their hands in the forearm pass position *(SEE FIGURE 53)*. To go to the right, they pivot on their left foot turn to the right, and step way out 90 degrees. Following that, they bend way down and try to scoop both hands under the ball *(SEE FIGURE 65-B)*. If they see they can't get both hands under the ball, they have to reach way out with the right hand, preferably palm down, and try to reach the ball. As they go down, whether they reach the ball or not, they bring the right knee down to the floor and turn it inward to their left. The left hand goes palm down close to in front of their right knee.

After that, they start to roll to their right and put their body on the floor *(SEE FIGURE 65-C)*. As they begin to roll, the put their left hand on their stomach, and keep the right arm extended. Next they roll on over towards the right onto their back *(SEE FIGURE 65-D)*, then keep rolling over that way until they are on their stomach. The second they get almost on their stomach, they put the left palm on the floor, get their right leg underneath them, bring the right hand in to the shoulder palm down, and push up to get quickly back to their feet *(SEE FIGURE 64-C)*. To go to the left, everything is just flip flopped or opposite.
Working the activity:
To practice this technique, first make sure they have their knee pads on. And it might be a good idea to get them some elbow pads to practice in. You can practice this out in the back yard where there is

some thick grass, or you can go out to a court someplace. First show, and explain to, your player what they will be doing. Next walk them through it slowly by the numbers then speed it up little by little until they appear to be catching on how to do it.

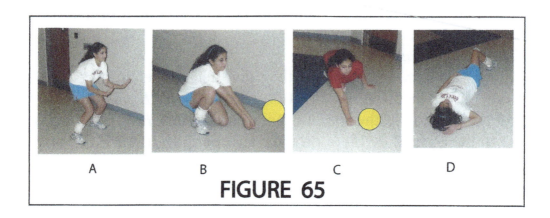

A   B   C   D

FIGURE 65

Step 1, have them get into the "ready" position *(SEE FIGURE 65-A)*. *Step 2*, they move the hands into the forearm pass position *(SEE FIGURE 53)*. *Step 3*, to go to their right, they take a big step about 90 degrees out to their right using the right foot. *Step 4*, they make a swinging scoop move out to their right with their hands *(SEE FIGURE 65-B)*. *Step 5*, they reach way out with the right hand, put their right knee down to the floor and rotate it inwards to their left, then put their left palm down as close as they can to in front of the right knee *(SEE FIGURE 65-C)*. *Step 6*, They roll over to the right onto their back placing the left hand on their stomach, and keeping their right arm extended *(SEE FIGURE 65-D)*. *Step 7*, They roll on over to the right so they are on their stomach placing the left palm down on the floor next to their left shoulder *(SEE FIGURE 64-C)*.

As they roll over, they pull the right hand in palm down on the floor, in front of their right shoulder.*(SEE FIGURE 64-C)*. The second they get both palms on the floor, they bring their right leg up underneath them, push up and get quickly to their feet. To practice going to the left, take the big step to the left and flip flop the procedure. They should make at least 3 moves to the right and 3 moves to the left at a training session.

Emphasize;

Learning how to make a quick decision on when to go down to their knees or stomach, to get a hand under the ball then getting their arms in the right place to make the roll over.

Run the Activity:

Run this activity quickly over and over for about 30 minutes.

Team Drill for Sprawl/Roll Over

This is a drill you can run with the whole team involved. You keep running this drill every once in a while to sharpen up the skills of all your players

The Sprawl/Roll Save Technique Drill (No.49)

Object of the drill:

Learn two techniques to reach out and save the ball. They are the sprawl and the roll. This drill will also be hard on the younger kids. You may want to wait until they have more experience, or they are 12 years or older

What you will need:

You will need a volleyball court with a net, a coach, a whistle, a cart of balls, a catcher, a feeder, and a shagger.

Working the drill:

Coach stands at the back lower corner of the court, then lobs the ball up in the air directly out in front of them towards the attack line. The lob has to be placed just right so that players need to do a sprawl or roll to reach the ball with one hand. If they can P1 saves the ball to the catcher, who rolls it to the shagger, who rolls it to the feeder. P1 goes to the end of the line. And P3 steps up. The feeder makes sure coach always has a ball ready.

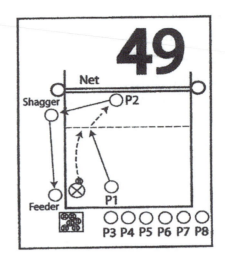

1. THE SPRAWL TECHNIQUE

First players try to get both hands under the ball for a forearm diving dig. If they can't, they try to reach out with the right hand, preferably with the palm down, if they need to go to the right. As they dive out and go down on their stomach, they put the side of their right knee on the floor, slide the right foot out to the right. At the same time they put their left hand down on the floor at their left side, and reach out for the ball. If they need to go to the left, everything is flip-flopped or opposite. To get up quickly, they push up with the left hand, slide the right knee back underneath them, and get to their feet. The left hand out is just the opposite.

2. THE ROLL TECHNIQUE

First they try to get both hands under the ball for a forearm diving dig. If they can't, they reach way out, preferably with the palm down, going underneath the ball. As they start to extend out and go down, they bring their right knee down to the floor and turn it inward to their left. The left hand, palm down, goes down close to and in front of the right knee. After that they start to roll to their right, and put their body on the floor.

As they begin to roll, they put their left hand on their stomach, and keep their right arm extended. Next they roll on over towards the right onto their back. Then they keep rolling over that way until they are on their stomach. When they are almost on their stomach, they put the left palm on the floor, get their right leg underneath them, bring the right hand in to the shoulder palm down, and push up to get to their feet. The left hand out is just the opposite.

Emphasize;

Getting down low, diving or extending way out with the arm, and placing their hands in the right place to break the fall, and help them get up quickly. The ball is flipped up using the back of the hand, palm down.

Run this drill:

Run the drill until each player gets at least 2 attempts at each technique. After 30 minutes the group moves to the next station or starts a different drill.

10. Blocking/Rebounding Techniques

Blocking is a defensive technique used to stop a spike, or a ball traveling over the net, from getting through to score a point for the opponent. It involves being able to read the hitter's intensions, and timing of their jump. Taller players have an advantage when using this technique. However, shorter players can also be effective by learning how to deflect or slow down hard hit balls. The object of the "block" is jump up, and deflect the ball back into the opponents court in such a way that the opponent *can not* return the blocked ball. Some organizations in Youth Volleyball, have a rule that only one player can block. This is probably because some youth teams are not very good at scoring points, and would not be able to get the ball past 2 or 3 blockers right in front of them. A "block" takes place usually right at the net, with the blocker placing both hands up in front of them above the net to stop and deflect the ball. The blocker's hands have the fingers all spread apart to allow them a better chance to make contact with the ball. Blockers must stay away from the net far enough to not touch it, and stay off of the court centerline. Players may not touch the net, or antennas, except with their hair. A blocker ceases to be a blocker when they have jumped and returned to the floor. Only front row player are allowed to complete a block. There is a special "ready" position for blockers. In addition to coming straight at the net, there are 2 basic footwork movement patterns for blocking. They are the "slide step" and the "crossover step."

The rebound is a defensive technique to receive a high hard hit spike. Some coaches call it an open handed "dig". You could use the setting, or overhead passing, technique to receive a high hit, but the interlocked hands rebound technique gives you more control on the ball return.

Skill Activity No. 60, 61, 62, 63- The Blocking Technique
Object of the Drill:
Teach your players how to make blocks.
What you will Need:
You will need a full court with a net to work on, a bucket of balls, 2 coaches, and a whistle.

FIGURE 60

The Basics Are:

The first thing to learn in the blocking technique is, the "ready position" *(SEE FIGURE 60)*. The player stands back a little from the net, and faces it. The feet are shoulder width apart, and the knees slightly bent. The hands are raised up about head height, with the fingers all open and palms facing forward *(SEE FIGURE 60)*. In this semi crouched position, they have to be ready to go in any direction necessary. Also they have to really watch where the hitter is coming from.

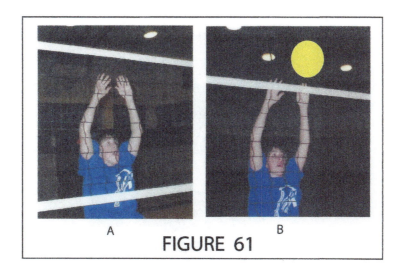

A   B

FIGURE 61

Next they would come straight at the net, slide step, or crossover step, to get into position across from the hitter to make the jump. As they begin the jump, the feet push up off the ground, and the elbows and knees extend. Next as they go forward and start to jump up in the air, they lock the elbows, bring the hands a little closer together, and keep the palms open. The forearms should be parallel to the net *(SEE FIGURE 61-A)*. Most of the time the blocker should time their jump just a little after the hitter jumps. The reason is, the hitter has to swing their arm after they jump. The timing is critical because if the blocker jumps too soon, they will be coming down as the ball starts to come over the net. Now they are up in the air.

They go up as high as possible, then tilt both wrists slightly forward just above the top of the net *(SEE FIGURE 61-B)*. The hand high as possible, then tilt both wrists slightly forward just above the top of the net *(SEE FIGURE 61-B)*.

The hand closest to the sideline should be rotated inward and away from the sideline. This is so that the ball will always deflect inside of the court and not go out of bounds. They want to try and make contact with the ball on the part of the palms right at the base of the thumbs *(SEE FIGURE 62)*. The fingers on both hands are spread and flexed (rigid). Explain to them that the hands have to be just back from the net far enough so that they don't touch the net.

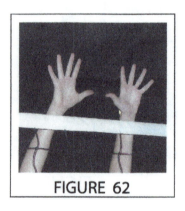

FIGURE 62

When they come down from the block, or attempted block, they should land on both feet and go immediately into the "ready" position again if the ball is still in play. A blocker who is shorter or one that can't get up to high in the air wants to make what is called a "soft block." This type of block deflects the ball somewhere in the blockers side of the court where it can be returned by a team mate. The difference is, the fingers are still spread but the wrists are tilted backwards to deflect the ball over their head or up in the air *(SEE FIGURE 63)*.

40

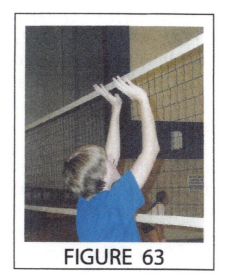

FIGURE 63

Working the activity:

To practice blocking you have to have a net. You can put one up out in the back yard, or find an open court somewhere. To start out, have your player get back about 3 to 4 feet away from the net, and face it. Next have them get into the "ready" position ***(SEE FIGURE 60)***. Now here is where is gets harder for you coach, mom, or dad. There are several ways you can set up this practice. First there is the *"stand and block"* method. This is where you, mom or dad, stand on a chair or some kind of platform across from them on the other side of the net. Then you push hit balls right at them. They can practice their "soft blocks" by staying right where they are. Make sure they tilt their wrists back though.

Now to practice the jump up blocks, have them run and jump up right in front of you on the chair. And when they get to the top of their jump, slam or push the ball hard right at their hands. Mix it up and have them come straight at you some of the time, then from one side then the other.

Watch them carefully and make sure they are using the "slide - step - slide" approach *(SEE SKILL ACTIVITY 27)*, or the "crossover step" approach *(SEE SKILL ACTIVITY 28)* for their footwork movements. For the little kids and beginners, you may want to lower the net or use a rope so that their hands can get up high enough to reach over the top of the net. Have them do at least 3 of these blocks at a training session.

The second method is the *"timing"* method to help them get their "timing" correct. To do this coach, mom, or dad, you will have to run up, jump, and spike the ball over the net. Mix it up, come from different places in the front row each time so that they get used to the ball coming at them from different angles. If you are not comfortable making the spikes, then get someone else to do them for you. This may be a better approach to the training because this way you can stand to the side and watch them more carefully. Probably the hardest thing to learn is going to be the "timing" part. They have to jump just a little after the hitter jumps so that their hands are right in front of the ball the instant it is hit. It will be a trial and error process until they learn. Also make sure they are getting right across from where it appears the hitters arm is aimed. Don't get discouraged and give up on them though because they can learn how to do this. Repetition, and correction, is the solution. Have them do at least 3 of these blocks at a training session.

The third method is a little more advanced for little kids and beginners. I am suggesting you work on this with 12 year olds and up. It is called the *"block - move - block"* drill. This is a little more advanced footwork technique to use. You, mom or dad, get on the chair or platform again. But this time move to about 2 or 3 feet in from the right sideline. Have your player get right across the net from you. Next spike or push hit the ball right at them. They have to try and block the hit. Right after they attempt the block, have them step backwards to the sideline. Then they immediately slide step back into position right across from you. Just as they get across from you, spike or push hit the ball at them again. This will happen quickly so you will have to have several balls ready. You may even need a helper to feed you another ball quickly. Next immediately after they make the block attempt, have them crossover step towards the far sideline one step then turn and crossover step back towards the near sideline. Then just as they turn and crossover step back, hit another ball at them. This drill is to teach them constant readiness and reaction to the ball. Have them do at least 2 groups of these near continuous blocks at a training session.

Emphasize;
Learning how to make a quick decision on where to go at the net to make the block.
Run the Activity:
Run this activity quickly over and over for about 30 minutes.

Skill Activity No. 66, 67- The Interlocked Hands Rebound Technique
Object of the Drill:
Teach your players how to use the rebound technique.
What you will Need:
You will need a full court with a net to work on, a bucket of balls, 2 coaches, and a whistle.
The Basics Are:
This technique requires the hands to be interlocked. The palms face forward above the head, with the fingers together. The right hand is placed behind the left hand, the thumbs are interlocked, and the wrists are tilted slightly backwards *(SEE FIGURE 66).*

FIGURE 66

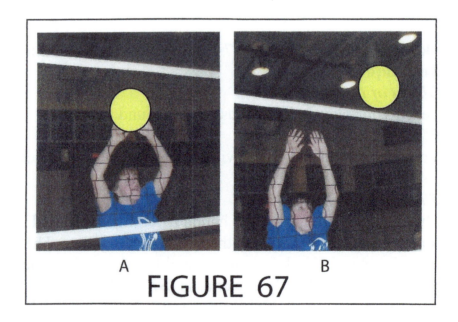

A   B

FIGURE 67

The player moves to the ball quickly, getting in front of it if possible. They try to maneuver so that the ball arrives in a position directly above their forehead, then they slightly bend their knees and elbows

(SEE FIGURE 67-A). They make contact with the ball either flat footed, or they jump straight up if necessary. The first contact with the ball is using the base of the palms, to deaden the impact. Then they try to "set' the ball up in air to a team mate *(SEE FIGURE 67-B)*.

Working the activity:

To practice this technique you can go out in the back yard where there is some thick grass, or you can go out to a court someplace that is open. You will probably need to have them bring a friend over to help out. First show, and explain to, your son or daughter and the friend what they will be doing. And then show your son or daughter what position their hands have to be in. Next walk your player through the moves slowly at first until they can master them correctly.

Start by having your player get into the "ready" position. Have them get out about 30 to 35 feet in front of you, mom or dad, or in the back row of the court. Have the friend stand just to the right of your player, and about 15 to 20 feet in front of them, and face them. Then you throw the ball hard, or hit it so that it comes right at your player just above their head. As you hit or start to throw the ball, have your player bring up their hands to the interlocked position *(SEE FIGURE 66)*. Next they get directly in front of the ball, tilt the wrists back, and bend their knees *(SEE FIGURE 67-A)*. Now what they want to do is determine how high the ball is, so they know whether to make contact by standing or jumping. They make contact with the ball on the base of their palms, try to deaden the balls impact a little, then "set" it up in the air to the friend in front of them *(SEE FIGURE 67-B)*. They should make at least 3 of these rebounds at a training session.

Emphasize;

Learning how to get in front of the hit and with their hands in the interlocked position.

Run the Activity:
Run this activity quickly over and over for about 30 minutes.

Team Blocking and Rebounding Drills

These are a drills you can run with the whole team involved. You keep running these drills every once in a while to sharpen up the skills of all your players

Basic Blocking Ready Position Drill (No.39)
Object of the drill:
Learn the basic ready position to get ready to make a block.
What you will need:
You will need half a volleyball court, and a net, 2 coaches, and a whistle.

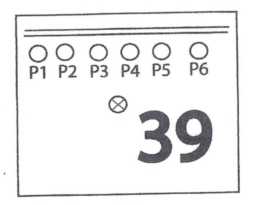

Working the drill:
This is a muscle memory drill to get players to automatically go to the ready position when they are about ready to make a block. Put 5 or 6 players up in the front row facing the net. Have them relax their hands down. Coach blows the whistle and all the players bring their hands up into the ready position.

Emphasize;

Getting the hands up and ready, squat down a little, and get the feet prepared to jump way up high.

Run this drill:

Run the drill until all players get at least 3 consecutive snaps to "ready" position. Rotate and switch players after the 3 snaps to the "ready position." After 15 minutes the group moves to the next station or start a new drill.

Standing Soft Block Drill (No.40)

Object of the drill:

Learn to make the standing still soft block.

What you will need:

You will need a volleyball court, a net, coach on a stand or chair, a whistle, a cart with balls, a feeder, and a shagger.

Working the drill:

This is a muscle memory drill to get players to automatically go to the ready position when they are about ready to make a soft block. One player P1 stands up in the front row in front of the coach. Coach yells, "Ready," and P1 brings their hands up in the ready position. Coach hammers a ball hard right towards their head. P1 makes a soft block, lets the ball go, then quickly gets set for the next block.

Emphasize;

Getting the hands up and ready, squat down a little and get set for the block. Feeder keeps handing coach balls, to keep the drill moving.

Run this drill:

Run the drill until all players get at least three consecutive soft blocks. Rotate and switch feeder, and shagger, after 9 blocks. After 20 minutes the group moves to the next station or starts a new drill.

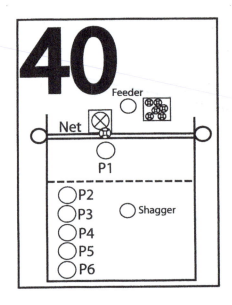

Single Player Block Drill (No.41)

Object of the drill:

Learn to make the block on a hitter.

What you will need:

You will need a volleyball court, a net, a cart with balls, a quick setter, a hitter, and a shagger.

Working the drill:

This is a muscle memory drill to get players to automatically learn to time their jump up and hands positioning. One player P1 stands up in the front row away from the net a little. Coach blows a whistle, setter makes a short quick set to the hitter, who tries to spike the ball right at the blocker. The blocker tries to time their run up and jump so that their hands are right in front of the ball and the hitters swing through hand. Setter always has a ball ready to quick set so that the drill keeps moving. Give the blocker three consecutive tries.

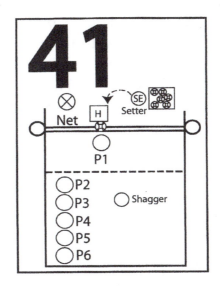

Emphasize:

Blockers need to work on their timing and hands position so that the ball is in the middle of both extended hands as they go up in the air. Thumbs and index fingers point to 1 or 11 O'clock. Coach can stand off to the side and observe their technique.

Run this drill:

Run the drill until all players get at least three consecutive blocks. Rotate and switch setter, and shagger, after 9 blocks. After 15 minutes the group moves to the next station or start a new drill.

Double Team Block Drill (No.42)

Object of the drill:

Learn to make the double team block on the opponent's best hitter.

What you will need:

You will need a volleyball court, a net, a cart with balls, a quick setter, a hitter, and a shagger.

Working the drill:

Before you work on this drill make sure it's legal in your league.

This is a muscle memory drill to get two players to automatically learn to time their jump up and hands positioning. Players P1 and P2 stand up in the front row away from the net a little. Coach blows a whistle and setter makes a short quick set to the hitter, who tries to spike the ball right at the blockers. The blockers try to time their run up and jumps so that their hands are right in front of the ball and the hitters swing through hand. Setter always has a ball ready to quick set so that the drill keeps moving. Give the blockers three consecutive tries.

Emphasize:

Blockers need to work on their timing and hands positioning so that the ball is in the middle of both their inside extended hands (centered) as they go up in the air. Coach can stand off to the side and observe the blockers technique.

Run this drill:

Run the drill until all two player pairs get at least three consecutive double team blocks. Rotate and switch setter, and shagger, and maybe the hitter, after 9 blocks. After 15 minutes the group moves to the next station or start a new drill.

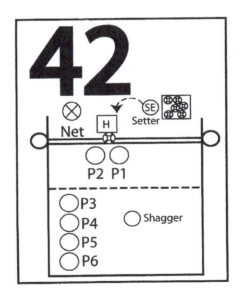

Blocking Footwork Drills (No.43)

Object of the drill:

Learn to make the correct footwork to get quickly in position to go up for the block. There are two variations for the footwork, the "pop over" and the "crossover" step.

What you will need:

You will need a volleyball court with a net, a hitter, 2 coaches, and a whistle.

Working the drill:

Which of these steps they use will depend on how far the need to get over to cover the hitter. The hitter can start in the center then move to where coach wants them. Have players start on the left side and move to the right, then next go to the right side and move to the left. On coache's whistle, the hitter moves to where coach wants them, jumps up, and fake swings a hit. Coach tells P1 which step to use, to get to a position in front of the hitter, where they would go up to block.

VARIATION 1- THE POP OVER STEP

P1 lifts their lead leg, jumps up off the trail leg, then lands on two feet at shoulder width apart.

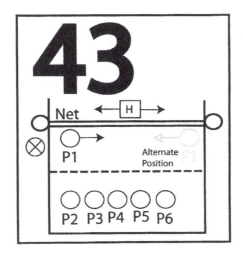

VARIATION 2- THE CROSSOVER STEP

P1 opens their lead leg in the direction of the block, next they cross over with the trail leg, close the lead leg then square their body to the net. As they do, they get booth feet off the floor to close. Blockers try to time their footwork move to get right in front of the ball and the hitters swing through hand.

Emphasize:

Blockers need to work on their footwork quickness and timing to get in position to make the block. Very important! Coach can stand off to the side and observe the blockers technique.

Run this drill:

Run the drill until each player gets one try going right, and one try going left, for each of the footwork steps. Rotate and switch the hitter, after 8 footwork moves because they will be getting tired. After 30 minutes the group moves to the next station or start a new drill.

Block-Move-Block Drill (No.44)

Object of the drill:

Learn to make the correct footwork to get quickly in position to go up for the block then make the block.

What you will need:

You will need a volleyball court, a net, a cart with balls, a coach on a platform or chair, a feeder, a whistle, and a shagger.

Working the drill:

This is going to be a tough drill for the younger kids. You may want to wait until they are 12 or older? Coach stands on the platform or chair a few feet in from the side line, and at the net. P1 lines up across the net from coach. Coach spikes the ball at P1, who attempts to block it. Then they let the ball go and side step to the near side line, then pop over step back to in front of coach, who spikes the ball at them again.

They attempt to block then let the ball go and crossover step towards mid court, then crossover step back to in front of coach. They spike the ball at them again, they attempt to block it. Then the whole process starts over again. After two blocking cycles, P1 goes to the end of the line. All through this the feeder keeps giving coach a ball. Next player P2 step up into place then they go through two cycles again. Make sure all players get their two blocking cycles.

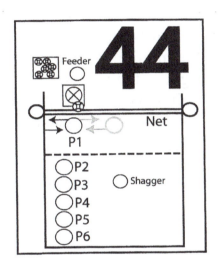

Emphasize;
Blockers using quick footwork and keeping hands up as they get back in front of coach.
Run this drill:
Run the drill until each player gets their two cycles. After 30 minutes the group moves to the next station or starts a new drill.

Blocking Skills Review
Common errors that need correcting
- Not penetrating the net.
- Failure to jump in close causing block to point out of bounds.
- Improper distance from the net.

The Rebound Technique (No.50)
Object of the drill:
Learn to receive a high hard hit spike.
What you will need:
You will need a volleyball court with a net, a cart with balls, a coach on a stand or chair, a whistle, a feeder, and a shagger.
Working the drill:
First coach demonstrates the technique with the hands interlocked, palms forward. Put three players P1, P2, and P3, in the back of the front row, facing towards the net. Coach stands facing them on a stand or chair in the middle of the other side of the net. They throw or hit balls hard right at the players. The player rebounds then gets ready for the next hit. Coach mixes up where hits go. Feeder has the next ball ready for coach. Give each player three rebounds, then rotate players.

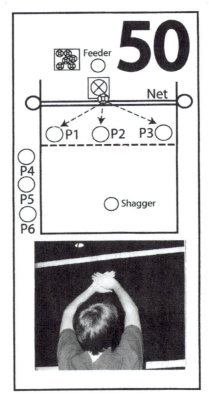

Emphasize;

Interlocking the hands correctly, getting them in front of the ball, and using the base of the palms to deaden the impact.

Run this drill:

Run the drill until each player gets at least 3 rebounds. After 15 minutes the group moves to the next station or starts a different drill.

11. Pursuing and Saving Techniques

This is probably a lost art with some players. And it may be because no one has trained them in this technique. Pursuing and saving is the act of chasing after wild or loose passes and catching up to them (the pursuing) before they hit the ground, the floor, or land out of bounds. This usually involves using the "sprawl," the "roll," or a dive and "dig," technique. When the player catches up to the ball they try to pass it to the nearest team mate (the save). There are other techniques they can use, depending on where the ball is in relation to them. If a high ball comes in, they can turn their back to the net and make a "reverse forearm pass" *(SEE FIGURE 68)*.

FIGURE 68

When a team mate can see you are about to "pursue" and attempt to "save" a ball, they should try to move into a position to receive your save. Lots of the time, kids will just stand around so to speak, and just watch the "save" attempt, rather than try to help. It's a matter of training. If you teach them by repetition, it becomes a "habit" and "muscle memory" with them.

Skill Activity No. 69, 70- Pursuing and Saving
Object of the Drill:
Teach your players how to pursue and make saves.
What you will Need:
You will need half a court with a net to work on, a bucket of balls, 2 coaches, a whistle, a feeder, and a shagger.
The Basics Are:
Players should pursue the ball in a running position with their hands apart *(SEE FIGURE 69)*. As an example, if they try to run with their hands in a "rebounding" position, it's going to slow them down getting to the ball. As they get close to the ball, they should move their hands to the forearm pass "platform" position *(SEE FIGURE 57-A)*, except keep the platform parallel to the ground. If the ball is above and over their head, they should turn their back to the net make a "reverse forearm pass."

If the ball is dropping fast way out in front of them, they should use the "sprawl" or the "roll" technique for the save. And occasionally they may even have to make a running, diving, dig save attempt *(SEE FIGURE 70)*. I am _not_ advising you to have the little kids attempt this. They could get hurt. And when they do practice diving for the ball, make sure they have knee and elbow pads on. It's probably better to wait until they are 12 years old or more before having them work on the diving technique.

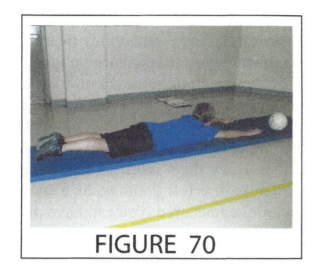

FIGURE 70

FIGURE 69

Working the activity:

To practice these techniques you coach, mom, or dad, will have to find someplace in the back yard or park with soft spongy grass, or go to a court or gym where they have pads they can land on. This is for safety reasons.

Start out by having them practice the "running forearm dig" pursue technique. Have them go out about 20 feet away from you, on the grass or the pads. Then you say "GO" or blow a whistle, then take the ball and underhand lob throw it low just a few feet in front of them. When they hear you say "GO" or the whistle they start to run towards you. It's going to be trial and error as to just when to reach out and make a platform "dig" save *(SEE FIGURE 57)*. For this particular technique training, have them reach and stay on their feet (no dive). At this point have them just try to get to the ball, and get their hands under it. Have them work on this technique at least 3 times at a training session. Once they have the technique mastered, you can have one of their friends there to receive the save.

For practicing the "sprawl" save technique, have them go out the same 20 feet away from you. Say "GO" or blow a whistle and make the same underhand lob throw towards them. When they hear "GO" or the whistle they start to run towards you. Make sure you throw it far enough away from them that they have to go down on their knee and reach for the ball. Again at this point have them just try to get to the ball, and get their hand under it *(SEE FIGURE 64)* . Then immediately after going down and reaching out, have them recover and get back quickly to their feet. Have them work on the "sprawl" to the right at least 2 times, then to the left 2 times, at a training session. Once they have the technique mastered, you can have one of their friends there to receive the save.

For practicing the "Roll" save technique, have them go out the same 20 feet away from you. Say "GO" or blow a whistle and make the same underhand lob throw towards them. When they hear "GO" or the whistle they start to run towards you. Make sure you throw it far enough away from them that they have to go down on their knee and reach for the ball. Again at this point have them just try to get to the ball, and get their hand under it *(SEE FIGURE 65)*. Then immediately after going down and reaching out, have them recover, roll over, and get back to their feet. Have them work on the "roll" to the right at least 2 times, then to the left 2 times at a training session. Once they have the technique mastered, you can have one of their friends there to receive the save.

For practicing the "dive and dig" save technique, have them go out the same 20 feet away from you. Say "GO" or blow the whistle and make the same underhand lob throw towards them. When they hear "GO" or the whistle they start to run towards you. Make sure you throw it far enough away from them, that they have to dive and reach for the ball with both hands out in front *(SEE FIGURE 70)*. Again at this point have them just try to get to the ball, and get their hand under it. Then immediately after going down and reaching out, have them recover and get back to their feet. Have them work on the "dive" to the right at least 2 times, then to the left 2 times, at a training session. Once they have the technique mastered, you can have one of their friends there to receive the save.

Emphasize:
Learning how to make a quick decision on how to pursue and make the save..

Run the Activity:
Run this activity quickly over and over for about 45 minutes.

Team Pursuing and Saving Drills

These are a drills you can run with the whole team involved. You keep running these drills every once in a while to sharpen up the skills of all your players.

Pursuing and Saving Technique Drill (No.51)
Object of the drill:
Learn to use a number of different ways to pursue and save the ball.

What you will need:
You will need a volleyball court with a net, a cart with balls, a coach on a stand or chair, a whistle, a feeder, and a shagger.

Working the drill:
First coach demonstrates, goes over, or reminds players of all the techniques they can use, and how to apply each method. Place 3 players in the front and back rows. On the whistle coach hits or throws the ball to spots in between the players, like in a kill situation. Players need to pursue and save the ball just like in a real game. Go continuous for 7 minutes, rest a few minutes then go for another 7.

Emphasize;

Players working as a team to defend against the hits. Players need to cover their teammates going down to save balls so that they can also get to their teammates instead of standing around and just watching.

Run this drill;

In 7 minute increments. After 30 minutes the group moves to the next station or start a different drill.

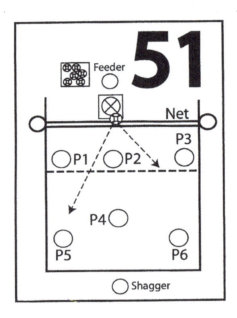

12. Defensive Plays and Group Tactics

Having a great defense is what separates average teams from great teams. You could have the best hitters and scorers in youth volleyball, but if they can't play defense, they won't win many games. Most youth coaches spend most of the practices working on offense because that is what kids like to do. If most of them had their way that's all you would do in practice is make hits and spikes. Defense is digging, blocking, saving and transitioning. Digging is a lot harder than passing for a setter. When your team is serving, it's going to depend on your defense as to whether you score the point or not. On rallies, most of the time your team is going to be playing defense. So why not learn to be good at it. Defense is about where to go and how to play your position. Teach them all the techniques for blocking, digging, sprawling and rolling. Impress on them to use teamwork to get the job done. When teamwork is working, the game is really going to be a lot of fun. Start out keeping it simple (K.I.S.S.), then as they get better and you can see progress in their skills, your defense can get more intricate.

Simple Basic Individual Tactics

Digging Tactics (No.200)

The first thing to determine is what type of attacking system is your opponent always using. Do they only use front row attacking, or do they only use back row attacking. "Back row" attacking and the "off speed" attacking techniques are quite different than a simple front row attacking system. A back row attacking system is usually harder to stop. The ball can come in higher, which makes it difficult to dig. What you need to do is teach your back row players to play deeper than normal so that they a few extra seconds to handle the ball. The front row players not involved in a block should get in position near the attack line and get ready to cover their blockers.

Blocking Tactics (No.201)

Tell your blockers not to jump up at the same exact time the attacker does because if they do they won't block the ball. Have them hold off a split second before jumping to increase their chances of getting their hands on the ball. Also their hands need to be tilted forward so that the ball goes downward off the block. They need to be wary of hitters trying to roll the block to the side off their hands. The counter is twisting their hands the opposite way of the roll off. Teach them to be ready for an off speed attack, which is tipping. And watch the ball, not the player or their wild arm swings.

Sprawling, Saving and Rolling (No.202)

This is really a timing and awareness technique. Back row players need to follow the ball, and check out which way the hitter is looking and aiming. Your middle back player needs to come up right behind the attack line, and behind their blockers, to cover tips and balls off the block. Then be ready to dive after any balls that get away off of the block. Once they get their hand under a dropping ball, they use a sprawl or rolling technique to quickly get back to their feet. Your left and right backs need to move back and towards the corners so they can cover hard hit balls from a back court attack. The weak part of a defense is the middle deep part of the court. Right and left backs need to be ready to slide and dive over to save balls coming into that part of the court.

Play Movement

No Blocking Defenses

5-1 Defense (No.73)

This is like the five player "W" receive pattern. All players are in similar positions then they shift a little. Your setter is at the net to give the diggers a target. The general areas the diggers are responsible for are within the dotted lines. If the ball is hit between two players, the one moving towards the setter digs the ball. The only difference between this defense and the regular receive pattern is the players all need to be lower to the floor and step to the ball, and they need to carefully read the hitters from within their areas.

Advantages
1. This is the safest defense for the younger smaller kids because there is no blocking. Less risk of injury.
2. This is one of the easiest defenses for the younger smaller kids to learn because it gives them the best chance for success.

Disadvantages

1. When you start playing against teams that can hit the ball hard from above the net, it will be much harder the dig the ball. At that time you may need to switch to a defense that includes blocking.
2. At some point, maybe in their teens, your players will probably outgrow this defense.

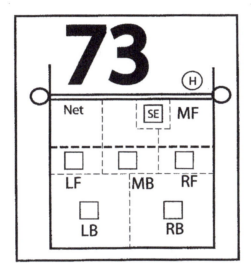

With Blocking Defenses

Note: If your kids are not teenagers yet, and they can't get their hands above the top of the net, don't use one of these blocking defenses.

Constant Back Court Hits Defense (No.74)

This is a defense to use when your opponent thinks they see a weakness then employs a constant back court attack. The ball comes over the net hard, and goes deep making it hard to dig. Front row players need to learn to be patient.

Advantages

1. This is easy to teach, so young teams could counter with this defense.
2. When front row players not involved with a block stay back near the attack line, and stay low, they have a better chance to reach blocker deflected balls.
3. If your back row players stay deep, they have more time and a better chance to handle the hard hit deep balls.

Disadvantages

1. When your blockers jump up to block too soon, which young kids like to do, they will miss the high hard balls coming over the net. Have them delay a split second before they jump up, it will give them a better chance at getting their hands on the ball.
2. If the back court defenders creep up too close to the attack line, they will have a hard time digging hard hit balls because they have less time to react.

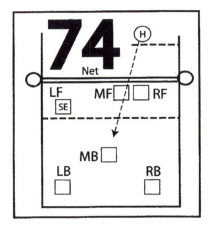

Constant Off Speed Hits Defense (No.75)

This is a defense to use when your opponent thinks they see a weakness then employs a constant off speed attack. The ball just tips over the net, and catches front row players by surprise and out of position.

64

Advantages

1. The middle back player is in a good position right behind the attack line to get to deflections and balls tipped towards the side line.
2. By moving closer to the corners, the right back and left back are in a better position to defend the rest of the court.

Disadvantages

1. There is a weak spot deep and in the middle of the court.
2. If the back court defenders creep up too close to the attack line, they will have a hard time digging hard hit return balls because they have less time to react.

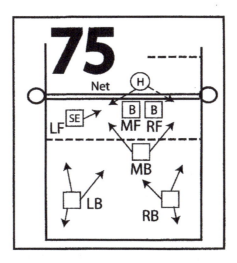

1-1, 2-2 Transitional Defense (No.76)

This is a transitional defense to use when your kids are 13 or 14, and just starting to learn how to block. It lets some kids block and others to stay down on the floor. At this age it is unusual to have a team where all the kids can get above the net. This is a bridge between a no block defense and a regular two player blocking defense. One blocker is at the net.

The other two front row players drop back to right on the attack line. The back row setter plays in the middle just above the attack line. The other two back court players split the back court, each one defending half the court. The blocker slides back and forth right at the net, ready to block. The setter has to cover and dig short tips and deflections. It's pretty simple really. If another front row player digs the ball, the setter releases to their target area to set up the attack.

Advantages

1. This defense lets you use your taller kids.
2. It distracts opposing hitters, who may not yet be used to having a blocker in front of them.
3. Its a balanced defense that does not have many holes for your opponent's to attack.

Disadvantages

1. When only one blocker is used at the net, they need to decide which hits to block and which hits not to block.
2. If the hit does not need a block, the blocker backs off the net and plays defense. When the blocker backs off, the setter releases immediately to the target area. This may take time to teach, and can confuse the blocker and setter.

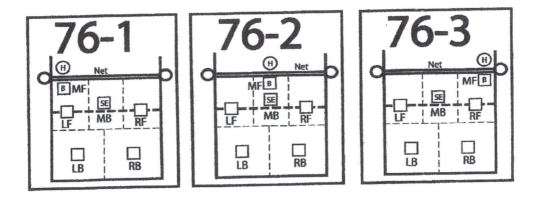

The Rotational Defense (No.77)

The rotational defense is designed to have two blockers right in front of the point of attack. The other four players rotate to a predetermined position on the court. These four players move from a basic starting position to a defensive position based on the direction of the opponent's set and where the hitter is located.

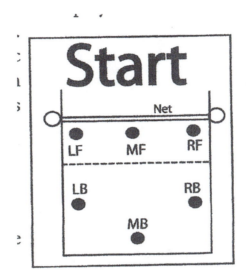

Advantages

2. This defense keeps the players moving and concentrating on the hitter. There are no players standing still.

Disadvantages

1. This defense will not work with slow players, or players that can not pay attention.
2. If the blockers can not make an effective block, holes will open up.

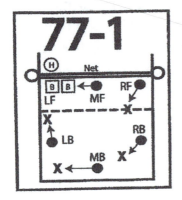 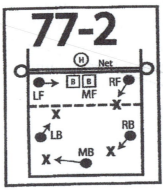 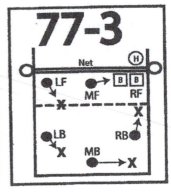

The Perimeter Defense (No.78)

This defense is designed to cover the middle of the floor. If you have a young team, you could use it, but it works better going against an experienced opponent. Many young teams don't cover the middle of the court to well. What this defense does is cover the boundary areas of the court, then use either your best defensive middle back or a "libero" to cover the whole middle area of the court.

They need to be a player that excels in digging and keeping rallies going. If your league allows a libero, and you have one, use them with this defense. The back corners of the court are usually the most exposed. This defense covers them. This may not be a good defense for a young team to use because you may not have a talented enough middle back.

Advantages

1. Against a good team hits and tips are covered, and so are the deep corners.
2. This defense takes advantage of using a libero.

3. If you have one good strong blocker, you can use a single blocker and relieve some of the defensive pressure and stop off speed attacks. This lets you transition quicker into your offense.

Disadvantages
   1. If you use just one blocker it makes it easier for hitters to find an open lane.
   2. If you use just one blocker it tests your team's communication skills.
   3. If you use just one blocker it weakens your defense against the big hitter if your opponent's have one.

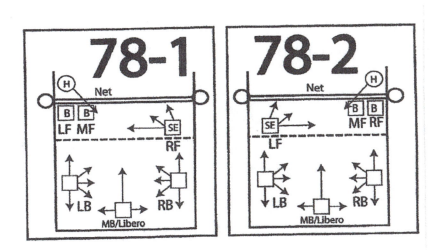

The Free Ball Defense (No.79)
This is a defense to use against a young team that is not big enough yet to power spike over the net. Free balls are usually hit soft, high, and deep. A block is not effective against a free ball. So what you do is deploy your players in more of a spread alignment. Have your left and right front players pull back off the net to just in front of the attack line, to cover all balls falling in front of them.

Your middle front player is your setter they cover any middle short balls, and get ready to set for your return attack. Any balls going deeper than the attack line are covered by your back court players. They balance the court with each one responsible for covering one third of the back court area.

Advantages
1. With this defense you don't need blockers, have your players just stay back in their positions and play defense.
2. This is a safe defense for a young beginning team, and easy to teach.

Disadvantages
1. This defense does have a weak spot in the center middle of the court unless you have a great middle back at the position every rotation. If you can use a "libero" put them at middle back.

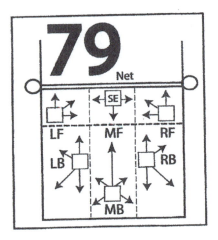

Using a Base Defense System (No.80)
This is a little different type of defense. Your team gets into a base defense position until your team captain determines whether the team should block or move into a free ball alignment. There are two base alignments to choose from, the 1-0-5 or the 1-1-4, before

moving to a 2-1-3 or a 2-4 alignment. When blocking, teach your players to observe the opposing hitters to see if they need more than one blocker. Use this rule; hitters that can't spike need only one blocker on them.

THE 1-0-5 BASE DEFENSE (-1)

Advantages
   1. With this base alignment your players don't need to move very far to cover deep hits during transition.

Disadvantages
   1. With this base alignment the middle, the net, tips, and short hits are vulnerable during transition.

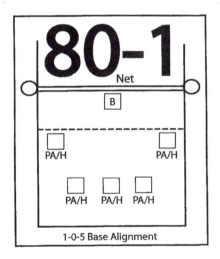

1-0-5 Base Alignment

THE 1-1-4 BASE DEFENSE (-2)

Advantages
   1. With this base alignment your players are in better position to cover short hits in the middle during transition.

2. With this base alignment your players are in better position to move to a double blocker defense during transition.

Disadvantages
1. With this base alignment the middle and the side lines are vulnerable during transition for a double block, depending on how your players shift.

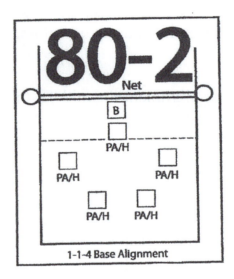

THE 2-1-3 BASE DEFENSE (-3)

Advantages
1. With this base alignment your players have the net covered for blocks, tips, short hits, and deep side line hits.
2. The whole court is covered better during transition, depending on players speed.

Disadvantages
1. With this base alignment quick cross court power hits are vulnerable during transition.

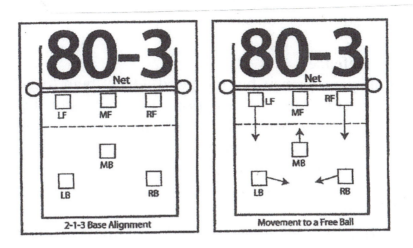

2-1-3 Base Alignment Movement to a Free Ball

Transitioning to Attack (No.81)

In volleyball your team needs to learn to transition from defense to attack very quickly. The more efficient your team is on setting up their attack, the more likely they can score a point. If your team is not able to efficiently transition into their offense, they will be forced to return a free ball to their opponent's. And when they keep doing this they are constantly on defense and unable to score. To keep this from happening, keep working them on their skills for forearm passing, digging, overhead passing, and hitting. Don't spend your entire defensive practice just on formations. Another problem is standing around, not communicating, just watching on defense. They need to call out, "Mine" or turn away so there is no confusion.

13. Defensive Strategies

Simple Common Sense Strategies

The first strategy I recommend is "have a game plan" to match the team you are playing. Remember though these are only kids, so coach accordingly with your strategies.

You know the old "KISS" (Keep-It-Simple-Stupid) phrase. Here are some basic strategies you can use:

For Boys Defense

1. If your team is not too good, teach them to get to the ball quickly, then make a good forearm pass or dig on the ball, then have them pass the ball around the maximum number of touches then hit it over the net. This is a slowdown tactic, and it will waste some time keeping the game closer. They may lose, but at least the point differential won't be as bad.

2. If your team is fast, teach them to pass or dig one touch to your setter, then to the spiker and over the net as quickly as possible before the opponent's can set up.

3. If your team is basically bigger, taller, and stronger than your opponent's, keep good spikers up in the front row and teach them to spike the ball around blockers, or between the two opponent's in front of them.

4. If your league allows a "libero," use them. They are defensive specialists. They add another dimension to your defense because they can replace any player in your back row without it counting as a substitution. Something to look into and think about.

5. Last fit your style of play to the players you have, and their skill level. Don't force your players to play a style you like, but their defensive skills don't fit into. You may get your way, but your team won't be successful or have fun. A recent survey of high school and lower level kids came up with this answer when they were asked, "Rate what the main, and most important, reason you came out to play volleyball was." Their number one, or near the top, answer was, "To have fun."

For Boys Special Teams
 1. Develop your special teams. Look for 9 potential starters. Have 6 good starters, then 3 substitutes for them by position. The rest of your team should be made up of specialists who have one or two outstanding skills, have the capability to directly score points, change the game momentum, or prevent your opponent's from gaining a momentum.

For Girls Defense
 1. If you have a team of young players that are not too good on defense, have them use a more settling technique. More ball handling, passing, using the maximum amount of touches, then spike the ball over the net. In other words a slower more deliberate offense. Have them maintain possession of the ball as long as possible, that way your opponent's can't score as often. Slow the game down! At least it will probably slow down the scoring and keep the game closer. Your opponent has to score to win games. This is even more important if your team is not too good at scoring.
 2. If your opponent's don't have good blockers, you can change your strategy a little. Have your good blockers up in the front row then teach them to aggressively block all the opponent's attempts to spike the ball. Keep the pressure on them!
 3. If you have a smart, fast, well trained, ball handling team you can use a lot of digs, and quick sets to your front row spikers to overwhelm your opponent's.
 4. If your team is bigger, taller, and stronger than your opponent's, go to an attack strategy right away. Keep good spikers up in the front row, focus on teaching them how to do all the spikes then go after your opponent's.

5. If your league allows a "libero," use them. They are defensive specialists. They add another dimension to your defense because they can replace any player in your back row without it counting as a substitution, something to look into and think about.

6. Last fit your style of play to the players you have on defense, and their skill level. Don't force your players to play a style you like they won't be successful or have fun. Is that what you want? A recent survey of high school and lower level kids came up with this answer when they were asked, "Rate what the main, and most important, reason you came out to play volleyball was." Their number one, or near the top, answer was, "To have fun."

For Girls Special Teams

1. Develop your special teams. Look for 9 potential starters. Have 6 good starters, then 3 substitutes for them by position. The rest of your team should be made up of specialists who have one or two outstanding skills, have the capability to directly score points, change the game momentum, or prevent your opponent's from gaining a momentum.

More Defensive Strategies and Player Responsibilities

There are many strategies for defensive volleyball. We are not going to attempt to explain each one to little kids, beginning coaches, and parents. What we will try to do is define what your player will be doing on defense to utilize the skills you have just practiced, and what responsibilities the different positions basically entail. It's the responsibility of the defense to stop the opponents from scoring points. Defense is what wins games. It takes a lot of time and practice to play good defense. In volleyball, players are on the court for offense and defense most of the time.

It changes back and forth every time the ball goes over the net. The most important skills for defense are "moving to the ball" and "digging." Work on these with your player, and make sure they keep improving on these two skills. When they get to their first team, their coach will decide which defense they will use. Make sure your player generally understands the responsibilities of each position, and the basic defensive patterns and formations.

Basic Defensive Player Responsibilities

The Middle Blocker:
It is the middle blockers responsibility to block anything in the front row middle part of the court. They also have to be able to quickly move to the left or right front row, to help a team mate on a "double block." When they are in the back row, they have to be digging and passing the ball. They have to be an aggressive boy or girl, that has a sense of protecting in their character. They have to be a good jumper, and have the capability to play way up high above the top of the net. When they transition to offense, they must be an excellent setter if they stay in the front row middle position. This has to be a boy or girl that is not the shy or timid type. They have to be very agile, to move back and forth, and get up in the air.

The Outside Blocker:
It is the left and right front outside blockers responsibility to block the opponents outside spikers and hitters. They have to be very aggressive like the "middle blocker," and have most of the same responsibilities. They must be excellent spikers and hitter when they transition to offense.

Defenders:
These are the back row players. It is their main responsibility to "move to the ball," "dig," and "save" the hard hit balls, in the middle and back part of the court.

They are the "grunt" and "grinder" type players. They don't get much recognition, but if they are good at this position they can stop the opposition from scoring points. They also have to be excellent passers, and setters, when they transition to offense.

The "libero" Defensive Specialist:
This a specialist position, and fairly new to the sport of volleyball. Most youth teams don't have this position. And many High Schools don't allow this position. Some teen age youth teams do allow this position. It has been in use in International, collegiate, USA Volleyball, and club level play for several years now. CYC (Catholic Youth Council) teams in St. Louis, Mo. do not allow this position when I last checked. I am mentioning it though because in some states, the High Schools are talking about adding it. And because it's used Internationally, it will eventually be used all over in the USA.

The "libero" is an option that may be exercised by one or both teams in the match. They wear a contrasting uniform to the rest of the players on the team, so they can be easily identified. They are allowed to replace any player in the back row only, without counting as a substitution. The use of the "libero" does not effect substitution or entries on either team. Their responsibility is defense and serve reception. They have to be excellent at digging out balls. They have to be able to go to the floor on sprawls, rolls, and dives.

When they transition to offense, they must be quick and have excellent passing skills. And they have to be able to hit from the back row, as long as they don't go above the net. They can not serve though. There can be only one "libero" at a time, designated for the entire game. There is no limit as to how many times they can come in or go out. They are in the game most of the time unless they get hurt. In that case, they have to be replaced by the player they replaced. Then a new "libero" is designated.

14. Team Learning Games

These are learning games you can have your team play once in a while. This will break up your practice from what seem to young players like endless hours of monotonous drills. While playing these games your kids are learning a core training skill, and having a little fun.

The Block Out Game (No.84)
Object of the game;
To make a block on the other teams hitters, and try to keep it inbounds on the attackers side of the court.
Goal;
To improve on your players blocking accuracy and techniques.
The game basics are :
This is a competitive game. You will need a volleyball court, either indoors or outdoors. Play 4 vs 4 on teams. Each team has a setter and two blockers at the net. The blocks can be single or double. The hitters on the receiving team must try to spike the ball into the front court. The rally is played out, points are given for blocks. Have a coach or parent keep track of the player's score on a pad of paper.

Give 3 points for a block that remains inbounds on the attackers side of the court. Give 2 points if the block keeps the ball from going over to the defenders side of the court. If the spike does not go into the front court, and a dig can not be made because the ball goes cross court, the serving team gets 1 point. The first team to get 20 points is the winner.

Playing the game :
Players stand back at the end line and try to serve the ball over the net. Team "A" serves to team "B." Three players stay at the net on each team. The player on team "B" not serving comes up and plays middle back on the receiving team.

The server on team "A" comes up and plays middle back after serving. Play is continuous. Alternate serves between the teams, no matter who wins the rally, one side then the other. Make sure each team gets an equal number of serves. Rotate the players, just like in the game, after each rally. Any player on the receiving side can be a setter or a blocker. The 3 players at the net move around any way they like, to try and get the block or spike. The middle backs make all the digs.

To make the game easier :
Lower the net. Or play 5 vs 5 or 6 vs 6.

To make the game harder :
Only give points for blocks that remain inbounds, and stay on the other side of the net. Or play 3 vs 3.

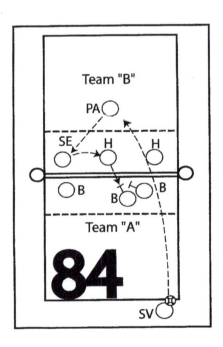

The Four Square Game (No.85)
Object of the game;
To make a block into a square on the other side of the court, then move up a square and end up at square No.1.
Goal;
To improve on their blocking accuracy and techniques, to get to the ball.
The game basics are :
This is a competitive game. You will need a volleyball court, either indoors or outdoors. Mark 2 squares on each side of the net use tape or cones. The 10 foot attack line is out of bounds line. There is a player in each square. When a block is not made correctly, the player making the mistake goes to the end of the line, then every player behind them moves up one square.

Playing the game :
The player in square No.1 starts the game by tossing the ball into any square on the opposite side of the net. The player in that square must block the ball into any square on the opposite side and within bounds. If the block falls on the blockers side, they go to the end of the line, and players move up one square. Players need to make a good block to stay in one of the squares, and avoid going to the end of the line. The player in square No.1 always rotates to the end of the waiting line. Coaches make sure the players hustle and keep the game moving. It's to a player's advantage to keep the game moving, and stay in one of the squares. The player that either stays or ends up in square No. 1 after playing 30 minutes wins the game.

To make the game easier :
Lower the net for the younger kids. Or make 3 squares on each side.

To make the game harder :
When the tosser starts to toss the ball, coach yells out a square number that the block must go into.

As an example, if the toss from square 1 goes to square 3 coach would yell, Number one," which would probably be harder for the blocker to get the ball into than square No. 2.

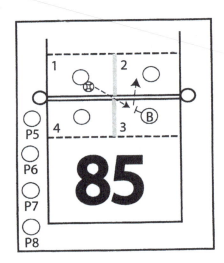

Wall Passing Shuttle Game (No.86)
Object of the game;
To make a pass into a square marked way up on a wall, then go to the end of the line while the next player steps up and passes it up in the square without the ball hitting the ground. Team tries to see how long they can keep it going from player to player.

Goal;
To improve on their passing accuracy and quickness to get to the ball.

The game basics are :
This is a fun game that involves teamwork. You will need a volleyball and a wall, either indoors or outdoors. Mark a 12 inch or 18 inch square up on a wall with tape. Depending on the size of your kids, the bottom should be about 3 - 4 feet over the top of their head.

Playing the game :

The first player in line stands about 4 feet away from the wall and starts it out by passing the ball up into the square, then gets quickly out of the way and goes to the end of the line. Mark a line 4 feet away from the wall with tape. The next player in line quickly moves up, catches the pass then immediately passes it back up into the square without it falling to the floor. This keeps going on from player to player until it falls to the floor. It will take teamwork to keep it going up. You can even have the player making the pass call out its number so that their teammates can tell the consecutive number of passes that have been made. The passes can be forearm or overhead.

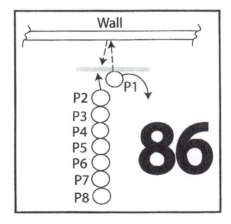

To make the game easier ;

Move a little closer to the wall for the little kids, and lower the square a little.

To make the game harder ;

Move a little farther away from the wall. Players can only use a forearm pass.

Down and Up Digging Game (No.92)
Object of the game :
Start one meter in from the end line, receive a long pass just in front of them, then dig the ball over a rope suspended over the attack line. And also try to dig it over the net for a point.

Goal;
To improve on their digging accuracy and technique, and the ability to get to the ball, place the dig where they want it to go, getting it cleanly over the net.

The game basics are :
The game is played 2 vs 2. Receiving team players line up 1 meter in from the end line at the starting line. A rope is held up 6 feet to 8 feet in the air, over the top of the attack line by coaches, parents, or players, and parallel to the net on both sides of the court. Have a coach get a pad of paper and keep track of the score

Playing the game :
Player P2 on one team starts the game by toss serving the ball over the net so that it lands just in front of the starting line, and the player receiving it has to move forward to dig it. Their dig must get over the rope on their side, and into the opponent's side. If they get the ball over the rope to the opponent's side they get 1 point. If the toss goes past the starting line it is considered out of bounds, and the ball goes over to the opponent's to toss. The player receiving the ball must stay behind the starting line until after the ball has been hit so that they are forced to dig the ball. When working with the younger kids, coach may need to stand on a platform and toss the ball to the player that will dig the ball because younger kids may not have the skills to place the ball where it needs to go.

Once the dig gets over the net, both teams start to rally just like a regular game and same rules. The rally play does not need to go over the rope though. So the players holding the rope can move it up next to the net where it will be out of the way until the rally ends, then move it back. Alternate the toss side when the rally is over, regardless of who wins the rally. Rotate the players on each team after the rally ends. Make sure each team gets an equal number of serve tosses. Play the game to five points then move on.

To make the game easier or more continuous :
Lower the net and rope for the younger beginning kids. Increase the number of players.

To make the game harder :
Continue regular play after the dig point has been made, then go to regular point type scoring. Move the starting line for the dig farther back.

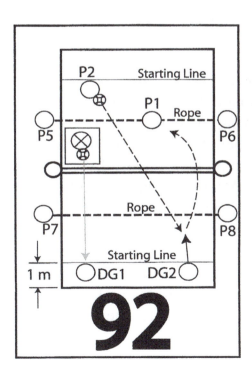

The Digging Relay Game (No.93)
Object of the game;
To dig a ball dropped over the net, get up race to the other side of the court, touch your teammates hand and go to the end of the line. Players try to dig and scramble quickly so that their team wins.

Goal;
To improve on their digging technique, and speed to get to the ball.

The game basics are :
This is a little relay game between two teams. Split up into two teams. On team is on one side of the net and the other team is on the opposite side of the net. Put half of the team on one side line and the other half on the opposite side line in equal numbers. You will need a volleyball court, two carts full of balls, two coaches to toss the balls, and two shaggers. Coaches start out by tossing balls out just a little ahead of the charging players in each line, who dig the ball, get up, and go tag their teammate.

Playing the game :
On coaches whistle the players need to charge out straight ahead, get down low, and dig the ball away from the net, then move across the court and tag their teammate on the opposite side. Tell them they need to get down on their knees, dive, or whatever they need to do to get to the ball. After they dig the ball they just let it go, then move across to tag their teammate. If they miss the dig badly they need to go back and do it over. When tagged the teammate then charges out, digs the ball, and goes to the end of the line on the far side of the court. This just keeps repeating then until coach blows their whistle ending the game. This will take a lot out of your players, so just play the game for 10 or 15 minutes then move on to another drill.

To make the game easier;
Coach can get closer to toss for the younger kids, where they just need to get low or on one knee to make their digs.

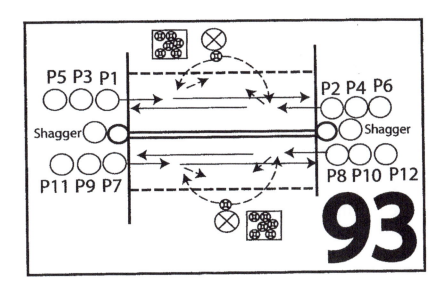

To make the game harder;
Coach can move farther away, and toss the ball out far enough ahead of players where they may need to dive every time to get under the ball.

The Elevation Game (No.505)
Object of the game;
Players need to jump straight up vertically to grab a flag. The idea is to keep jumping as high up as they can.
Goal;
Get players to jump up higher to make blocks.

The game basics are :
This is a little game where all players take turns to develop their ability to jump straight up as high as they can to grab a flag on a broom, stick or pole held by coach.

Playing the game :
All players line up to the side of the net. One player at a time goes to the center of the net. Coach gets a pole or broom handle, and hangs a flag, handkerchief, or rag over the tip of the pole or broom. Then they go stand at the end of the net on a stand or ladder. Coach starts out by raising the flag to a height that all players, standing directly underneath, can easily jump up and reach. Then after once through the line, coach raises the flag a little higher each time through the line. They keep doing this until only one player can jump up high enough to gab the flag. That player wins the game.

To make the game easier;
Coach can let the little kids get a running start to their jump.

To make the game harder;
Coach makes all players stand flat footed under the flag before they jump.

The Balloon Game (No.305)
Object of the game;
Two players hit a balloon back and forth to each other over the net, and try to keep the balloon from hitting the floor

Goal;
Improve on their ability to move around to get to the balloon.

The game basics are :
This is a little game between two players hitting a balloon back and forth over the net to each other. Each player tries to get to the balloon and hit it back over the net to the other player. They want to get to the balloon and hit it back over the net. You will need a big heavy duty balloon for this to work. Or they can use a light weight balloon and just tap it lightly.

Playing the game :
Split the team up into two lines, one on one side of the net and one on the other side. On coaches whistle, two players start hitting the balloon back and forth over the net to each other. You can start out by letting each pair get 3 to 5 minutes playing, then rotate players. They can play longer if you like, it will depend on how many players you have. If you are playing this game over a net in the backyard, I would play no longer than 5 minutes with the little beginning kids. Then give them a rest.

To make the game easier;
If the little beginning kids can't keep the balloon from dropping to the floor or ground let them pick it up and start over hitting it back and forth.

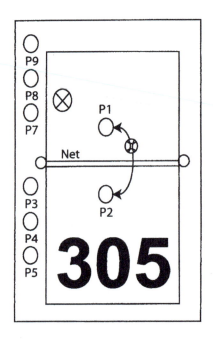

To make the game harder;
If a player lets the balloon hit the floor they are out of the game and a new player replaces them. Then they go to the end of the line. A new player then moves up to take their place and the game begins again. Each player gets to play until the balloon hits the floor on their side of the court.

The Rebound King Game (No.306)
Object of the game;
Learning how to rebound an air ball over to a team mate.

Goal;
Improve on their ability to rebound the ball to another player.

The game basics are : This is a little game to see who is the best rebounder. Coach stands on a chair or ladder at the end of the net and throws the ball in the air to a player in the middle of the court.

90

Using open hands or locked hands they need to rebound the ball in the air to a target player.

Playing the game :
Split the team up into two lines, one on one side of the net and one on the other side. One player goes to the middle of the court. The target player goes up close to the net or wherever you want them. You can play both sides of the court to speed the practice up. Let each player get 3 rebound chances, then rotate players. After their 3 chances they go to the end of the line. Award 1 point if the player can rebound the ball close to the target player, Award 2 points if they can rebound the ball just over the head of the target player. Have a shagger. The target player rolls the ball over to the shagger, who gives it to the coach. Play the game for about 30 minutes. Have a assistant coach or another player get a pad of paper and a pencil to keep track of the points each player has. Make sure the target players get to rotate and have their chance to rebound. Play the game rapidly so that the players get more chances. At the end of the time period the player with the most points wins the game and becomes the "Rebound King."

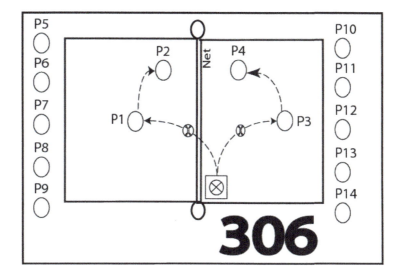

To make the game easier;
Coach lobs the ball over to the little kids, and the target players are brought in just a little closed to the rebounder.

To make the game harder;
Players must rebound the ball to just over the head of the target player in order to get any points.

The Sprawl King Game (No.307)
Object of the game;
Learning how to get better at sprawling to get to hard hit balls that are away from them just out of their normal reach.

Goal;
Improve on their ability to use the sprawl technique to rebound the ball to another player.

The game basics are : This is a little game to see who is the best sprawler. This is very similar to the "Rebound King" game. Coach stands on a chair or ladder at the end of the net and throws the ball in the air just out of the reach of a player in the middle of the court. Using the sprawl technique they need to rebound the ball in the air to a target player.

Playing the game :
Split the team up into two lines, one on one side of the net and one on the other side. One player goes to the middle of the court. The target player goes up close to the net or wherever you want them. You can play both sides of the court to speed the practice up. Let each player get 3 sprawling rebound chances, then rotate players. After their 3 chances they go to the end of the line. Award 1 point if the player can rebound the ball close to the target player, Award 2 points if they can rebound the ball to where the target player can reach it or just over the head of the target player (ideal). Have a

shagger. The target player rolls the ball over to the shagger, who gives it to the coach. Play the game for about 30 minutes. Have a assistant coach or another player get a pad of paper and a pencil to keep track of the points each player has. Make sure you rotate the target players so that they get their chance at a sprawling rebound. Play the game rapidly so that the players get more chances. At the end of the time period the player with the most points wins the game and becomes the "Sprawl King."

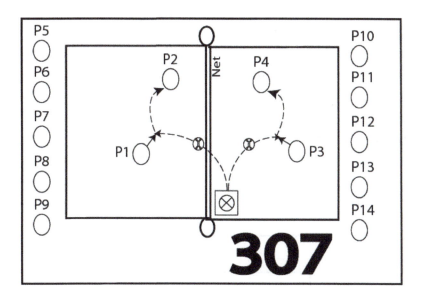

To make the game easier;
Coach lobs the ball over to the little kids, and the target players are brought in just a little closed to the sprawling rebounder.

To make the game harder;
Players must rebound the ball to just over the head of the target player in order to get any points.

The 4 On 4 Volleyball Game (No.308)
Object of the game;
Learning how to play the game with fewer kids on the court and with more touches.

Goal;
Improve on their ability to play volleyball by getting more touches without so many players on the court.

The game basics are :
This is played just like a regular volleyball game except with only 4 players on a side. For the young beginning kids you may also want to relax the rules just a little.

Playing the game :
I would play the game for only 30 minutes then put in 8 new players. Have the 8 new players ready so that the transition is quick letting more players get real game type experience during practice.

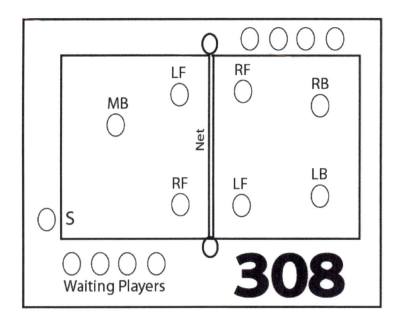

To make the game easier;
Play only 20 minutes and relax the rules.

To make the game harder;
Use the regular rules and play to a regular score end.

15.Sample Practice Schedules

Practice Rituals

Closing Ritual (No.106)
Object of the information:
To help your kids feel a sense of closure after practices and games.

Why Have a Closing Ritual:
The "Positive Coaching Alliance (PCA)," of which I am a member, recommends this as an end to practices. This is a brief gathering where coaches and players signify the end of the days activity, and provide a transition back to life without sports. This is a time to remind them of the next practice, or a coming Game time and date. Make sure you let them know they did a good job during the day's practice. And last everyone puts their hands up in the air together in the center of the group and on the command, "Ready," they all together yell "Yeah Team," or something like that. Your kids will know what to say.

Practices

Practice Schedules (No.107)
Object of the information:
To stress the importance of setting up a practice schedule to get more training in during practices.

Why Have Practice Schedules:

When you lay out a practice schedule, kids learn more, and faster (Practice is usually 1 hour for beginners). You can't always follow it to the letter, but try to follow it as close as possible within reason. I know many of you coaches don't like to follow a schedule, but if you do, you are going to find that the young kids learn a lot more. It makes the learning process quicker, and their skills improve much faster. The secret is plan out what you want to teach each session then get some assistant coaches to help. First thing to do is get yourself a dedicated to volleyball calendar. Mark all your practice dates and times down for a master schedule, then make copies and give them to your players. I want to point out something here my practice schedules are not etched in stone, The practice schedules I am showing are just for giving you some ideas on how to plan them. Also make sure you have practice cancellation telephone number to call in case it is necessary.

Coaches

Get as many as possible. They can even be parents, who may just be sitting around doing nothing all the way through practice while just watching anyway. Might as well put them to work, it's not hard if you just show them exactly what it is you want them to do. I do this all the time. And I find that many parents are willing to help as long as you show them EXACTLY what it is you want them to do. We will put some different types of one hour sample schedules together for you to see some different ways how to do it. The idea is to show you how to teach larger groups the same fundamentals in 2 days instead of maybe 3 or 4. If you can only get on the practice court 1 or 2 days a week, then see if you can find a gym with a net open someplace to get extra practices. Young kids need lots of practice to really learn the fundamental better. There is a lot more to learn when you don't have much practice time.

Practice Area

A lot of these drills can be run out in a grass area. Some Leagues will only let you practice 2 times a week when school is in session. During the summer, many youth teams practice every day if possible and they can find the space. Typically teams will work with the nearest School program to share their court. I think it's best to work on a full size court with a net if you can find one. When you work with the local School, they will also usually let you share their equipment, as long as you take care of it. They will also have lights so that you can work after dark. It gives you lots more options.

Practice Schedules

We will take the middle of the road and show some sample 1 hour schedules for you to look at. They are based on evening practices with the younger kids. The time can always be adjusted for day practices or other times. They are also based on half your team practicing offensive fundamentals, while the other half works on defense.

1 Hour Sample Schedules
METHOD 1- BEGINNERS
(Group of up to 15)

Practice 1 (One Coach, Two Assistants)
The ***Focus is on Blocking***

Whole Group Altogether
4:30 to 4:35. Jumping jacks to loosen up
4:35 to 4:40 Warm Up and Stretching
　　　　　　Whistle blows to go to First Station

Coach Plus Assistants (Whole Group)
4:40 to 4:55 The blocking technique

4:55 to 5:00 **Water Break** Whistle blows to start and end
5:00 to 5:30 The interlocked hands rebound technique
          Practice ends with a whistle
5:30 to 5:35 Short Talk and Closing Ritual

Practice 2 (One Coach, Two Assistants)
The *Focus is on Blocking*

Whole Group Altogether
4:30 to 4:35. Jumping jacks to loosen up
4:35 to 4:40 Warm Up and Stretching
          Whistle blows to go to First Station

Coach Plus Assistants (Whole Group)
4:40 to 4:55. The blocking ready position
4:55 to 5:00 **Water Break** Whistle blows to start and end
5:00 to 5:15 The single player block drill
5:15 to 5:30 The double team block drill
          Practice ends with a whistle
5:30 to 5:35 Short Talk and Closing Ritual

METHOD 2- BEGINNERS
(Group of up to 20)

Practice 1 (One Coach, Three Assistants)
The *Focus is on Digging*

NOTE: Split into Two Groups (Stations)

Group 1, 2 Altogether
4:30 to 4:35. Jumping jacks to loosen up
4:35 to 4:40 Warm Up and Stretching
          Whistle blows to go to First Station

Coach Plus Assistant Station1 (Up to 10 Kids)
4:40 to 4:55 The dig technique with Gp.1
4:55 to 5:00 **Water Break** Whistle blows to start and end
         Whistle blows to Rotate Group to next Station (No.2)
5:00 to 5:30 The partner digging drill with Gp.2
         Whistle blows to gather for End of Practice
5:30 to 5:35 Short talk and closing ritual (All together)

Asst.No.1 Plus Assistant Station 2 (Up to10 Kids)
4:40 to 4:55 The dig and cover drill with Gp.2
4:55 to 5:00 **Water Break** Whistle blows to start and end
         Whistle blows to Rotate Group to next Station (No.1)
5:00 to 5:30 Scramble dive and dig save drill with Gp.1
         Whistle blows to gather for End of Practice
5:30 to 5:35 Short talk and closing ritual (All together)

Practice 2 (One Coach, Three Assistants)
The ***Focus is on Digging and Blocking***

NOTE: Split into Two Groups (Stations)

Group 1, 2 Altogether
4:30 to 4:35. Jumping jacks to loosen up
4:35 to 4:40 Warm Up and Stretching
         Whistle blows to go to First Station

Coach Plus Assistant Station1 (Up to10 Kids)
4:40 to 4:55 The teamwork digging drill with Gp.1
4:55 to 5:00 **Water Break** Whistle blows to start and end
         Whistle blows to rotate group to next Station (No.2)
5:00 to 5:30 The sprawl technique with Gp.2 (Continued)
         Whistle blows to gather for End of Practice
5:30 to 5:35 Short talk and closing ritual (All together)

Asst.No.1 Plus Assistant Station 2 (Up to 10 Kids)
4:40 to 4:55 The blocking technique with Gp.2
4:55 to 5:00 **Water Break** Whistle blows to start and end
             Whistle blows to rotate group to next Station (No.1)
5:00 to 5:30 The roll technique with Gp.1
             Whistle blows to gather for End of Practice
5:30 to 5:35 Short talk and closing ritual (All together)

METHOD 3- BEGINNERS
(Groups of up to 21)

Practice 1 (One Coach, Five Assistants)
The *Focus is on Blocking, Digging, and Sprawling*

NOTE: Split into Three Groups (Stations)

Group 1, 2 ,3 Altogether
4:30 to 4:35. Jumping jacks to loosen up
4:35 to 4:40 Warm Up and Stretching
             Whistle blows to go to First Station

Coach Plus Assistant   Station1 (Up to 7 Kids)
4:40 to 4:55 The blocking technique with Gp.1
4:55 to 5:00 **Water Break** Whistle blows to start and end
             Whistle blows to rotate group to next Station (No.2)
5:00 to 5:30 The blocking technique with Gp.3
             Whistle blows to gather for End of Practice
5:30 to 5:35 Short talk and closing ritual (All together)

Asst.No.1 Plus Assistant Station 2 (Up to 7 Kids)
4:40 to 4:55 The dig technique with Gp.2
4:55 to 5:00 **Water Break** Whistle blows to start and end
             Whistle blows to rotate group to next Station (No.3)

5:00 to 5:30 The dig technique with Gp.3
              Whistle blows to gather for End of Practice
5:30 to 5:35 Short talk and closing ritual (All together)

Asst.No.2 Plus Assistant Station 3 (Up to 7 Kids)
4:40 to 4:55 The sprawl technique with Gp.3
4:55 to 5:00 **Water Break** Whistle blows to start and end
              Whistle blows to rotate group to next Station (No.1)
5:00 to 5:30 The sprawl technique with Gp.2
              Whistle blows to gather for End of Practice
5:30 to 5:35 Short talk and closing ritual (All together)

Practice 6 (One Coach, Five Assistants)
The ***Focus is on Blocking, Digging, and Sprawling***

NOTE: Split into Three Groups (Stations)

Group 1, 2 ,3 Altogether
4:30 to 4:35. Jumping jacks to loosen up
4:35 to 4:40 Warm Up and Stretching
              Whistle blows to go to First Station   (Continued)

Coach Plus Assistant Station1 (Up to 7 Kids)
4:40 to 4:55 The blocking technique with Gp.1
4:55 to 5:00 **Water Break** Whistle blows to start and end
              Whistle blows to rotate group to next Station (No.2)
5:00 to 5:15 The blocking ready position with Gp.3
              Whistle blows to rotate group to next Station (No.2)
5:15 to 5:30 The standing soft block drill with Gp.2
              Whistle blows to gather for End of Practice
5:30 to 5:35 Short talk and closing ritual (All together)

Asst.No.1 Plus Assistant Station 2 (Up to 7 Kids)

4:40 to 4:55 The dig technique with Gp.2

4:55 to 5:00 **Water Break** Whistle blows to start and end
                  Whistle blows to rotate group to next Station (No.3)

5:00 to 5:15 The partner digging drill with Gp.1
                  Whistle blows to rotate group to next Station (No.3)

5:15 to 5:30 The dig and cover drill with Gp.3
                  Whistle blows to gather for End of Practice

5:30 to 5:35 Short talk and closing ritual (All together)

Asst.No.2 Plus Assistant Station 3 (Up to 7 Kids)

4:40 to 4:55 The sprawl technique with Gp.3

4:55 to 5:00 **Water Break** Whistle blows to start and end
                  Whistle blows to rotate group to next Station (No.1)

5:00 to 5:15 The roll technique with Gp.2
                  Whistle blows to rotate group to next Station (No.1)

5:15 to 5:30 The sprawl/roll over drill with Gp.1
                  Whistle blows to gather for End of Practice

5:30 to 5:35 Short talk and closing ritual (All together)

METHOD 4- BEGINNERS

Later On Practice (One Coach, Five Assistants)
The ***Focus is on Team Blocking, Digging, and Sprawling Plays***

NOTE: Split into Three Groups (Stations)

Group 1, 2 ,3 Altogether

4:30 to 4:35. Jumping jacks to loosen up

4:35 to 4:40 Warm Up and Stretching
                  Whistle blows to go to First Station

Coach Plus Assistant Station1 (Up to 7 Kids)

4:40 to 4:55 The digging relay game with Gp.1

4:55 to 5:00 **Water Break** Whistle blows to start and end
     Whistle blows to rotate group to next Station (No.2)

5:00 to 5:15 Team blocking plays with Gp.3
     Whistle blows to rotate group to next Station (No.2)

5:15 to 5:30 Team blocking plays with Gp.2
     Whistle blows to gather for end of practice

5:30 to 5:35 Short talk and closing ritual (All together)

Asst.No.1 Plus Assistant Station 2 (Up to 7 Kids)

4:40 to 4:55 The digging relay game with Gp.2

4:55 to 5:00 **Water Break** Whistle blows to start and end
     Whistle blows to rotate group to next Station (No.3)

5:00 to 5:15 Team digging plays with Gp.1
     Whistle blows to rotate group to next Station (No.3)

5:15 to 5:30 Team digging plays with Gp.3
     Whistle blows to gather for End of Practice

5:30 to 5:35 Short talk and closing ritual (All together)

Asst.No.2 Plus Assistant Station 3 (Up to 7 Kids)

4:40 to 4:55 The digging relay game with Gp.3

4:55 to 5:00 **Water Break** Whistle blows to start and end
     Whistle blows to rotate group to next Station (No.1)

5:00 to 5:15 Team sprawling and rolling plays with Gp.2
     Whistle blows to rotate group to next Station (No.1)

5:15 to 5:30 Team sprawling and rolling plays with Gp.1
     Whistle blows to gather for End of Practice

5:30 to 5:35 Short talk and closing ritual (All together)

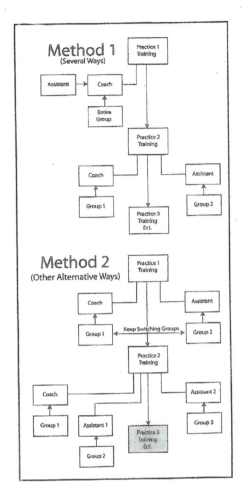

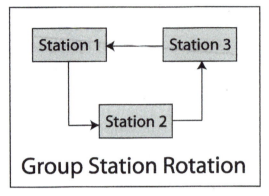

Group Station Rotation

Scheduling Summation

We have given you a bunch of different methods and ideas to help you make a schedule for your practice training. I know that many of you don't like to do this because I have talked to a lot of coaches over the years about scheduling. However, you need assistant coaches and parents to help you get better. If you can get them, you will see that things can go smoothly. You can also be innovative, and tailor the schedule to suit your own coaching style and techniques.

There is almost an infinite amount of combinations you can have. If your coaches don't like teaching the same thing for four straight 15 minute sessions, then mix it up and have each one of them teach something different at each 15 minute session at their station. However, tell them it is easier doing it three or six straight times because they don't need to change their court set up at every session. And they get a different group of kids each time, and each different group has their own challenges. So, if you don't like what I have shown then be innovative.

My only comment is don't try to do it all yourself. It does NOT work, especially if you have a big group. I hate when I happen to be out driving somewhere, and happen to see a big group of kids at something like a football practice just standing around waiting while coach only has one or two kids at a time over to the side trying to instruct them how to do something, and everyone else is just standing around doing nothing. In fact it does not even look like they are watching sometimes. There is a better way, if you will just try it.

THE END

CPSIA information can be obtained at www.ICGtesting.com
Printed in the USA
LVOW02s1415270414

383285LV00030B/15/P